GANGSTERS
& ORGANIZED CRIME
IN JEWISH CHICAGO

GANGSTERS
& ORGANIZED CRIME
IN JEWISH CHICAGO

ALEX GAREL-FRANTZEN

Charleston · London

THE
History
PRESS

Published by The History Press
Charleston, SC 29403
www.historypress.net

First published 2013

Manufactured in the United States

ISBN 978.1.62619.193.8

Library of Congress CIP data applied for.

To Mom, Dad, Anna and Adam

CONTENTS

ACKNOWLEDGEMENTS

A book would not be complete without thanking those who have helped me along the way. Ben Gibson and The History Press made this book—my dream—a reality. Their love for history runs deep, and it has been a true pleasure to work with them. I wish to thank Scott Bartlett for his guidance, Professor Liebersohn for teaching me research methodology and Professor Leff for serving as my second reader during thesis defense. I also would like to thank all the other teachers who have inspired me to imagine, create and learn throughout my life.

I wish to thank the great library staffs with which I have had the privilege of working: John Hoffmann and Ryan Ross at the Illinois History and Lincoln Collections; everyone at the Main Library who housed me for long afternoon and weekend hours; the University of Chicago Special Collections staff; and those at Spertus Library. I would also like to thank Dr. Joseph Kraus, who shares my passion for Jewish crime. Moreover, *Gangsters* would not be in print without the Chicago History Museum, whose brilliant collections and photographs helped bring to life this tremendous chapter in Chicago Jewish history.

I am forever indebted to my thesis group; they are an incredible group of individuals, and we supported one another the entire way. A special thanks to my editing partner, Xi Xi, for her thoughtful comments and critiques. Professor Symes led an inspiring thesis seminar and provided us with academic and emotional support through the darkest and lightest times of our journey together. I had the honor and privilege of writing *Gangsters* under Professor James Barrett's advisement; he is an exceptional historian and counselor and an even better person.

I would also like to thank my friends who were, as always, supportive of me as I researched, drafted and redrafted *Gangsters*. I would not be the person I am without you guys.

Brittany has been there for me every step of the way; we share in a semi-charmed life that I would not trade. Thank you for loving me and all my flaws as I worked through *Gangsters*.

Lastly, I wish to thank my family, both past and present. Thank you to Bub, Bill, Oll, George, Marshall and Estelle for paving our way and demonstrating why they are the greatest generation. Additionally, I would be nothing without Anna and Adam, who helped to raise me and shape who I am. I owe everything to my mom and dad, whose love, support and wisdom continue to guide me as I move forward in this adventure. And of course, thank you to our dogs, Molly, Max and Fenix, for keeping my lap and heart warm.

INTRODUCTION

In defense of them, they always were enterprising.
—*Shirley Garel*

Over the past few years, I have made a conscious effort to record conversations with my eighty-nine-year-old Jewish grandmother, Shirley Garel, and her ninety-one-year-old brother, Marshall Peiros. In 1921, when Marshall was just six months old, the Peiros family emigrated from Lithuania and settled near Columbus Park in Chicago—an area of second settlement for Jews. In the early spring of 2011, my great-uncle Marshall told a story that inspired the research for this book. "Do you know who Al Capone is?" he asked.

> *Well you know I was a very good ballplayer. So we were at Columbus Park and they* [the Capone family] *were from Cicero. The neighborhood we grew up in, there were very few Jews. It was Irish and Italian. So the Italian guys, I played ball with them a lot. So the Capone brothers, Matt and Ralph, every Sunday they'd come out to play ball and were both pitchers—you know, softball—and each had a team out, and we'd play against each other. So they invited me there and got me on Matt's team. Matt was the nicer guy. Ralph was a real rat. It was the fourth or fifth inning one day, and Ralph was pitching. All of a sudden, some guy gets a hit and slides into second—the ump calls him safe. So Ralph turns to the ref and slowly puts his hand in his pocket like he had a gun.*

"So I decided," he paused and laughed, "not to go back with those guys again."[1]

His brief memory opened my eyes to the intricacies of urban life and illuminated the level of interaction that existed between various ethnic groups on the streets of Chicago during the early twentieth century. If my great-uncle brushed up against the brothers of Al Capone, which other Jews dealt with the city's gangsters? At once, I became fascinated with the origins of the Jewish community and the intersection of Jews and crime. This study examines the role of crime in shaping the Chicago Jewish community. Broader still, it serves as an exploration of ethnicity and crime and as an addition to the understanding of the immigrant experience in American cities.

Most historians have focused solely on the role of other ethnic groups— Italian and Irish—in the Chicago underworld. Indeed, seminal works by authors like Herbert Asbury and John Landesco aided more in understanding the evolution of the broader Chicago gangland than in determining the impact of crime on the Jewish community.[2] However, scholars have given greater attention to Jewish crime and gangsters in other cities, and particularly in New York City, where their influence is well documented and researched. The work of Jenna Weissman Joselit of George Washington University stands out among the rest. Her book *Our Gang: Jewish Crime and the New York Jewish Community, 1900–1940* revealed the critical importance of crime in shaping New York Jewry. "Crime," she contends, "served to highlight New York Jewry's understanding of itself even as it shaped the outside world's view of its Jewish neighbors."[3] Her emphasis on crime as central to defining the New York Jewish experience provided a framework I could consider applying to the Chicago Jewish community and helped me to see the greater importance of criminal events. This book, in part, will serve as a source of comparison between crime's influence in New York and Chicago.

Historians like Mark H. Haller have explored the relationship between ethnicity and crime. In "Ethnic Crime: The Organized Underworld of Early 20th Century Chicago," Haller demonstrates that the underworld was a path of social mobility for immigrants and their children. Additionally, he illustrates that there were various ways in which each ethnic group came to participate in criminal activities and establishes that the underworld impacted, both economically and socially, Chicago's working-class ethnic communities. Haller's treatment of Jewish gangsters is brief. Though he underscores that social mobility served as a motivation for Jews, he does not explain how the values of the Jewish community or Judaism shaped these criminals. Haller's most intriguing claim is that the "entrepreneurial and professional services of Jews clearly reflected broader patterns of Jewish adaptation to American urban life."[4] However, this is a gross oversimplification of the Chicago Jewish experience. We will see that it was not a homogenous community but rather one marked by distinct waves of German and Eastern European Jewish immigrants—each bringing over particular community and religious values and varying inclinations to "assimilate."

Furthermore, it was essential for me to examine the historiography of Jews in Chicago. There are several scholars who have been instrumental in helping me grasp a firm understanding of the community's history and place my findings in a larger context, including Irving Cutler's *Jews of Chicago*, Louis Wirth's *The Ghetto* and Hyman Louis Meites's *History of the Jews of Chicago*. Most primarily focus on the achievements of the Jews—the institutions built, the growth of a vibrant culture and the rise of prominent community members. Nonetheless, what is most interesting about these works is what the authors seldom mention: the existence of crime in the Jewish community and the role it played in its development. Cutler writes, "Those few from the Maxwell Street ghetto who strayed into the criminal element were infamous more for the use of their heads than for the use of guns," which downplays the frequency and significance of vice in the West Side district.[5]

Of course, there were several important factors that shaped the Chicago Jewish community, many of which scholars have explored. In this book, I contend that in the early twentieth century, Jewish crime—from juvenile delinquency to labor racketeering—played a significant role in forming the Jewish community on Chicago's West Side and the neighborhood's character. Conversely, the physical, social and economic conditions of the Maxwell Street ghetto also produced this proliferation of gangsters. Crime's pervasiveness in the ghetto forced community members to make sense of and respond to the criminal behaviors of their brethren in relation to the value sets emphasized in their religion, culture and family life. Consequently, vice challenged and refined these principles. Moreover, crime brought out tensions between the city and the Jewish community, as well as rifts between Reform and Orthodox Jews. Respectively, then, it illuminated the gentile's perception of the city's Jews, and vice versa, while also shaping the identity of the West Side community.

Four principal questions and several corresponding, subordinate concerns focused my research and guided me toward demonstrating crime's great importance in the development of Chicago Jewry. First, who were the Jewish gangsters and what does this tell us about the situation of Jews in

Chicago during the early twentieth century? What were their motivations? Did the criminals tend to emigrate from particular countries? How did the environment of the Jewish community contribute to delinquency and what was their relationship to Judaism? Second, how did Jewish delinquents and gangsters relate to those of other ethnic groups? It was important to consider the interactions Jews had with their Irish, Italian and Polish neighbors because the mixing often occurred in public spaces and in the city's street gangs. Third, how and why did the position and image of the Jewish criminal change over time? Finally, how did the Jewish community relate and respond to their gangsters and the problem of crime? How did the community's organizations respond to and reflect on the Jewish delinquents and criminals? What was the role and perspective of the Yiddish newspapers?[6]

In order to understand how Jewish crime shaped Chicago's Jewry, the first chapter of this book relates the general history of how the community came to be and its subsequent development up until the turn of the century. It underscores the fundamental cultural and religious differences between the first and second—German and Eastern European—waves of Jewish immigration and the dynamic between the two groups. These variations afforded each group of Jews different degrees of social and economic mobility. In the case of the Eastern European Jews, a ghetto on the West Side emerged, and conditions there paved the way for crime to proliferate. The subsequent chapter centers on the streets of the Jewish ghetto and how its environment led youth down the path of juvenile delinquency and involvement in boys' gangs. The streets also exposed the children to surrounding ethnic groups, cultivating both positive and negative interactions, and introduced them to the realities of anti-Semitism. The youths' misconduct elicited varied responses and proposed solutions from the Jewish community. The third chapter considers the transition of these juvenile delinquents into organized crime and reasons for why some Jews made such a passage. Additionally, it introduces the reader to the Chicago underworld and how the Jewish ghetto fit into this landscape of vice and immorality.

The rest of the book analyzes Jews in various criminal ventures to demonstrate how their involvement impacted Chicago Jewry and how the community responded to the gangsters. Though interesting, I intentionally do not extensively discuss Jewish gangsters in organized crime outfits, such as Al Capone's Syndicate, because these figures were generally further removed from the Jewish community and did not directly reveal as much about the neighborhood. Indeed, this is not meant to be an exhaustive history of Jewish involvement in Chicago organized crime. Instead, I try to position myself closer to the streets, determining how the criminals and the voices of the city and Jewish community interacted and shaped one another. In turn, chapter four focuses on the extensive role of Jews in the white slave trade and the subsequent response from the Jewish community. It pays particular attention to the 1909 trial of police inspector Edward McCann and the surprising testimony and revelations of chief witnesses, brothers Julius and Louis Frank. Consequently, many leaders of the Jewish community took great initiative in the reform effort, in part, to fight against the detrimental effects such explosive involvement had on the reputation of the city's Jews. The following chapter surveys Jews in gambling by examining the crooked career of the ghetto's longstanding alderman, Emanuel Abrahams, as well as events at a particular gambling house on Maxwell Street—in the heart of the ghetto. Both studies serve to highlight the tensions between the Jewish community and the greater gentile population, seen through various perspectives expressed in English and Yiddish newspapers. Chapter six explores crime during the Prohibition era. More specifically, it concentrates on Jewish bootleggers and labor racketeers. Together, they exemplify how crime markedly impacted the marketplace, economy and labor movement in the Jewish community while also exposing the differences that remained between Orthodox and Reform Jews. Furthermore, they presented two contrasting faces of the Orthodox rabbis, redefined the perceived morality of Jewish religious leaders and ultimately reflected the increasing organization of the Chicago rabbinate.

This book revisits the formation of the Jewish community on Chicago's West Side during the first thirty-five years of the twentieth century through the eyes of crime. From poverty-stricken residents of the ghetto's tenements to corrupt rabbis, crime reached and affected all segments of the Chicago Jewish community. Of course, there were several critical factors that shaped this community. However, crime—an often forgotten and overlooked chapter in the history of Chicago's Jewry—was very significant to this process, just as it was for many other ethnic groups who settled in Chicago and in other major American cities at the turn of the century.

Chicago's Community Areas

A map of Chicago's community areas, including the Near West Side and various areas of second settlement. *Courtesy of the Newberry Library, Chicago, available at http://www.encyclopedia. chicagohistory.org/pages/1760/html.*

I

THE FORMATION OF THE CHICAGO JEWISH COMMUNITY

1838–1900

On the West Side…one can walk the streets for blocks and see none but Semitic features and hear nothing but the Hebrew patois of Russian Poland.[7]
—Chicago Tribune, *1891*

In 1833, at the time of its incorporation, the town of Chicago housed a few hundred people of "all nations and kindred and people and tongues."[8] The houses, primitive and hastily built, lay beside a boundless prairie and Lake Michigan. Yet Charles Butler, a New York financier, real estate broker and railroad promoter who visited Chicago that fall, recounted, "Even at this early day the experienced observer saw the germ of a city, destined from its peculiar position near the head of the Lake and its remarkable harbor formed by the river, to become the largest inland commercial Emporium in the United States."[9] It was this early setting—a future commercial center in its swampy infancy with great expectations—that enticed the first Jews, primarily from Bavaria, to settle in Chicago.

A study on Chicago Jewish crime of the early twentieth century inevitably conjures up images of men donning finely tailored suits and fedoras and of murder scenes lined with police tape. However, it is in the 1800s that this story finds its beginnings. By understanding the formation of the Jewish community in Chicago, with particular emphasis on the religious and cultural differences between the first and second waves of immigration, it will be evident how crime—both disorganized and organized—came to play a significant role in shaping the life of the Jewish community.

Lithograph depicting Michigan Avenue from the lake, 1866. *Chicago History Museum, ICHi-62074, Louis Kurz for Jevne & Almini.*

I

It is likely that the first Jew to settle in Chicago, J. Gottlieb, a Jewish peddler from Bavaria, arrived in 1838, when the population was just over four thousand people. He ostensibly proceeded to California in search of gold during the rush of 1849. Hyman Meites, a historian of the Chicago Jewish community, speculated that Peter Cohen, John Hays and Morris Baumgarten, appearing in the directories of the time, were Jewish contemporaries of Gottlieb in Chicago.[10] However, to many of these settlers, like Gottlieb, Chicago was not a destination but rather a stop in transit to California gold. Additionally, there is no concrete evidence that affirms they were Jewish—only conjectures based on the "Jewishness" of their names. By 1841, however, the first permanent Jewish settlers had arrived. Brother-in-laws Benedict Shubart and Philip Newburgh, both in their late twenties, started a merchant tailoring business on Lake Street, Chicago's primary business thoroughfare and the site where most early Jews established themselves. Though not on Lake Street, Isaac Ziegler and Henry Horner both started their own wholesome grocery stores.[11] Additionally, Horner would prove instrumental in the establishment of the Chicago Board of Trade in 1848.[12] Most of these early settlers, young men interested in peddling or merchandising, emigrated from Germany to evade the *Familiantenrecht*, family law that restricted Jews' right to marry and limited the number of Jewish families.[13] It was this kind of persecution that gave some German Jews an incentive to seek America and a burgeoning city of opportunity such as Chicago.

On the High Holiday of Yom Kippur in 1845, as more settlers came from Germany, the Jews of Chicago formed the city's first *minyan*—the required group of ten adult males for religious services. Jacob Rosenberg and Levi Rosenfeld held the services and subsequent important communal matters above their store at 155 Lake Street, which flourished "at a time when Marshall Field was a struggling clerk."[14] Though small in number, these early German Jews—now forming a tightly knit community—immediately sought to establish the essential institutions that characterized their life in the old country, i.e., the burial society and synagogue. In turn, 1845 saw the establishment of the first Jewish organization in Chicago, the Jewish Burial Ground Society (JBGS). However, the Hebrew Benevolent Society largely replaced the burial ground the JBGS had purchased in modern-day Lincoln Park because of environmentally undesirable conditions. Purchased in 1851, the new cemetery, a three-acre plot of land in the town of Lake View, would become the oldest Jewish cemetery in Chicago.[15] Additionally, as more relatives continued to arrive from Germany, the organization of a congregation became centrally important to the community.

In November 1847, at Rosenfeld and Rosenberg's store, when the Jews numbered fewer than one hundred in a Chicago population of roughly seventeen thousand, Kehilath Anshe Maariv (KAM)—"Congregation of the Men of the West"—was born. True to the name, all of the congregation's initial fourteen members were male. The all-German membership observed strict orthodox Ashkenazic ritual, including the separation of the sexes during prayer and the Sabbath.[16] The men first worshiped above the Lake Street store, but with a continual growth in membership, a separate site was constructed at Clark and Quincy Streets in 1851.[17] The augmented membership was the result of emigrants fleeing Germany following the Revolutions of 1848. Historian Bruce Levine estimates that between 1840 and 1860, roughly one and a half million Germans immigrated to the United States.[18] Scholars have suggested several reasons for this astounding figure. Some point to Germany's economic stagnation. Others suggest that it was the "disruptive effects of rapid industrialization," which contrasted with Germany's long tradition, when compared to Great Britain, of having a backward agrarian economy and a primitive society as a whole.[19] While these undoubtedly frustrated the Jewish population, the outburst of anti-Semitism during riots played a more significant role.[20] It appeared that the Jews were scapegoats for Germans agitated by their society's changing tides in the middle of the nineteenth century.

One of two prominent newspapers at the time, the *Chicago Daily Democrat*, wrote an article about the dedication of the new synagogue at Clark and Quincy Streets on June 14, 1851. Though it is evident that the Jewish customs fascinated the writer, he also provided us with an early perspective of the German Jew's place in Chicago. He penned, "The Jews in our city are not numerous, but are wealthy, very respectable and public spirited."[21] That the first Jewish settlers, largely Bavarians, had peacefully and successfully established themselves among the gentile communities in Chicago is of critical importance. It was because of this and the social mobility it afforded them that a Chicago Jewish criminal or gangster of German—more specifically, Bavarian—descent was rare in the twentieth century.

What followed in the second half of the nineteenth century was a complex history that relates the growing divisions and tensions within the Chicago Jewish community, illustrated primarily through the emergence of new congregations. In addition to the Bavarians, an increasing number of German-Polish Jews arrived from the Herzogtum Lauenburg ("Duchy of Lauenburg") district of Prussian Poland. The Bavarians, most able to now enjoy a higher standard of living, considered the Poles to be an "inferior caste."[22] In 1852, these Polish Jews, dissenting from KAM, which was now widely known as the *Bayerische Shul* ("Bavarian synagogue"), formed their own congregation: Kehilath B'nai Sholom. When compared to KAM, the new congregation was more Orthodox and utilized the Polish prayer book.[23]

Yet another, perhaps more significant, division soon emerged from within KAM. Members of this reform movement, emphasizing the progressiveness of Jewish law, believed that Judaism needed to be modernized. The reform, in turn, would allow the Jews to better adapt to society. This reflected the larger Haskalah movement, or Jewish Enlightenment, among Jews in Europe, which was an outgrowth of the general eighteenth-century European Enlightenment. Indeed the influence of the Enlightenment, compounded by economic developments and political upheavals of the 1840s, left a mark on Germany's Jewish minority.[24] Consequently, the Haskalah movement caught hold of higher-class Jews in Germany by the middle decades of the nineteenth century. This demonstrated that, though the divisions often occurred along religious lines, it was an equally social, economic and political movement toward Western integration. By 1859, unable to reach agreements, members of the Chicago Jewish Reform movement founded the Jewish Reform Society, and in 1861, they established the Sinai Reform Congregation.[25] Wirth notes that the existence of four Jewish cemeteries, three of which were side by side, was "an outward manifestation of the division that was beginning to characterize the Jewish community."[26] At the onset of the Civil War, the question of religious reform remained the most pertinent issue among the Jewish community. Moreover, it is important to note the locations of the Jewish population by this time. The older settlers had moved toward the south of the Loop, while the newer settlers resided in the area recently abandoned by these older settlers—the "western fringe of the Loop."[27]

II

Throughout the 1860s, the Jewish population continued to grow—a growth not just fueled by German Jews. Some emigrated from Holland while others came from Eastern Europe, particularly Latvia and Lithuania. The new Yiddish-speaking Jews from Eastern Europe brought with them traditions more Orthodox than those of the Germans and Poles, so naturally they soon established several synagogues, such as the B'nai Jacob.[28] However, the next significant events in the formation of the Jewish community prior to the second wave of immigration were the Great Chicago Fire of 1871 and what might be an even greater and far-reaching conflagration in 1874.

The Jewish population was approximately 4,000 in a city of 334,000 in the fall of 1871. The Jews now bolstered ten congregations and many more social organizations. Yet the fire on October 8, 1871, ravaged the German Jewish community—indeed, the city as a whole—because so many of these Jews worked and resided in the area the fire affected (the Loop) and because the majority of its structures were wooden.[29] The devastation was clear, but the response of the city and the Jewish community is more noteworthy. A genuine sense of optimism laced with determination emerged. The *Chicago Tribune* proclaimed on October 11, 1871, "The people of this once beautiful city have resolved that CHICAGO SHALL RISE AGAIN…The Christian world is coming to our relief."[30] However, the Jewish population also received help from both local Jewish relief organizations and Jewish communities across

An aerial view of the desolation following the Great Chicago Fire, Congress Street near Michigan Avenue, 1871. *Chicago History Museum, ICHi-68147.*

A *carte de visite* illustrating the legend of Mrs. O'Leary's cow and the start of the Great Chicago Fire, circa 1871. *Chicago History Museum, ICHi-50775, J.D. Pierce & Co.*

the nation. Despite this network of aid, the German Jews did not receive much help from the Russo-Polish settlers, who were largely spared by the Great Chicago Fire.[31] This sense of abandonment felt by the German Jews would kindle the growing tensions among the Jewish communities and significantly alter the aftermath of the second fire three years later.

The *Chicago Tribune* reported in its July 16, 1874 article entitled "The Fires," "The Israelite rag-shop, in the alley-way between Fourth avenue and Clark street, just south of Taylor street, was the place where the fire orginated [sic]. This shop was a little frame shed in the rear of Isaac Snur's grocery store, which was almost in rear of French's oil refinery, the inflammable stock of which was the first great cause of the spread of destruction."[32] Only three years later, another devastating conflagration ignited the city. This time it struck the near South Side and the Russo-Polish settlers, the poorest segment of the Jewish population, the hardest. The United Hebrew Relief Association attempted to respond, but it was unable to raise adequate funds. The German Jews were unwilling to help their co-religionists. They severely criticized the Russo-Poles for not coming to their aid after the Great Chicago Fire and wrote them off simply as *schnorrers*, Yiddish for "beggars."[33] Dr. Liebman Adler, former rabbi of KAM and highly regarded by all community members, wrote a plea to garner greater support. After acknowledging the widening physical, social and religious schism between German and Eastern European Jews, he implored, "These unfortunates [Russo-Poles] come to us from a country which is the European headquarters for barbarism, ignorance, and uncleanliness [sic]…In conferring charity it is the duty of the Israelite first to look at the needs and then to the deserts of the recipient."[34] The plea, coming from one of their own, ultimately mobilized the German Jews to provide the necessary funds, but largely out of pity.[35]

Furthermore, the 1874 fire led to a most critical geographical realignment of the Russo-Pole community. With all of their communal organs destroyed east of the river, the Eastern European Jews crossed the tributary to the near West Side. They replaced the Irish and German populations who could now afford to live in better areas of the city. The full significance of this relocation would not manifest itself until the second great wave of immigration flooded into the neighborhood a few years later. It would be in this new neighborhood on the West Side where the conditions ripened for Jewish crime, street gangs and vice to proliferate.

III

In 1881, the assassination of Czar Alexander II ended the welcomed reprieve from the customary harsh treatment the Russian Jews experienced.[36] The subsequent passage of the "May Laws" of 1882, a set of geographically and intellectually restrictive laws against the Jews, sparked a massive immigration movement to America. The unrelenting persecution that followed, including hundreds of pogroms, sustained this mass exodus from Russia. Though most settled in metropolises like New York City and Boston, many of the impoverished and distressed Jews pressed westward. In 1881–82, an estimated two thousand Jews came to Chicago.[37] In a mere decade, the Jews arrived to a city whose population doubled to over one million people—80 percent of whom were immigrants or their children.[38]

These Jews sought a section of the city where rents were cheapest and the reestablishment of their cultural life was possible. In turn, they poured into the near West Side, a most undesirable, filthy area but the obvious choice nonetheless—perhaps the only choice.[39] The Eastern European Jews "chose" the near West Side just as most newly arrived immigrant groups initially fall into the poorest sectors of an urban area. Eventually, these groups move into areas of higher social standing as they gain greater economic mobility, and in their place, a new ethnic group arrives. This pattern of movement was not unique to the Jews, then, but part of a general phenomenon.

There were several initial markers that distinguished these Jews from their predecessors. The men grew long beards and side-locks and wore the attire of their old country—long coats and boots. They spoke Yiddish, making communication with strangers and other Jews exceedingly difficult. Few possessed skills transferrable to work in the city's business district, and consequently, most engaged in unskilled labor and peddling.[40] It is critical to remember that they, unlike those before them, did not seek Chicago for economic opportunities, low cost of living or social mobility but rather for their personal safety and greater religious tolerance.[41] Indeed, the West Side Jewish community, inhabited in 1874 by the Russo-Polish Jews, increasingly became known as "the ghetto" and took on the character of the Russian pale—the *shtetl* (town).[42]

In order to understand the ghetto, it is important to first grasp the community the Russian Jews left, as they transplanted much of this culture to the New World. In 1791, the Russian government instituted the Pale of Settlement for the Jews, which restricted their residency to certain areas of the Russian Empire.[43] The Jews oftentimes kept to themselves in tightly knit *shtetlach* that fostered a distinct sense of identity among inhabitants. Their culture centered on the home, synagogue and marketplace. They followed an Orthodox code of laws that instilled in them certain religious beliefs, dietary regulations, ethical values and social duties.[44] On the West Side, then, these refugees sought to maintain their identity and lifestyle among those who understood the life of the shtetlach. Social worker and economist Edith Abbott correctly observed that this explained "the clannishness of the orthodox Jews…which kept them so long in segregated, congested settlements."[45]

The Chicago Jewish community saw it as their duty to help their poor co-religionists adjust to the new surroundings, but it was largely for self-serving reasons. The older settlers wanted to protect the reputation of the Jewish community that their hard work had afforded them. Though physically separated from the West Side settlement, the first-wave Jews on the South and North Sides grew increasingly uneasy over the ghetto's growth. Sociologist Louis Wirth noted, "They sensed that all the progress they had made in breaking down barriers, in preventing the development of a ghetto and in gaining recognition for themselves, as persons rather than as Jews, with their Christian neighbors might now…come to a sudden halt."[46] Remarkably, however, the Russian Jews also frowned upon their German brethren. After all, they were Reformed, "halfway" Jews and did not even comprehend the mother language of Yiddish.[47] In turn, divisions persisted, and the Russians continued to establish organizations, maintain their Orthodox demeanor and overcrowd the ghetto.

The synagogue at Canal and Liberty Streets became a sanctuary for the Orthodox Jewish culture the Russians kept, but the home, also a central part of shtetl living, was less than ideal in the ghetto. The old frame tenements were extraordinarily run-down and overcrowded. The streets were poorly paved, narrow and filthy.[48] Extreme cases found six family members sleeping in a single bed to allow space for the ten additional lodgers sharing the tenement.[49] Moreover, the ghetto was stricken with bad plumbing. An article published in the *Chicago Tribune* on July 19, 1891, titled "Our Russian Exiles: Views in the Hebrew Quarter on the West Side" provides an exemplary view into the extreme conditions of the ghetto. Concerning the plumbing, the article states, "There are a number of dingy-looking doorways, over which a sign proclaims that Russian baths may be taken within…But the Russian bath-houses have the appearance of neglect, which the condition of the inhabitants does not belie."[50]

Yet despite these dilapidated housing conditions, the Jews were able to develop the synagogue and the third integral component of the Russian shtetl: the marketplace. However, the marketplace limited most of the ghetto's inhabitants to a backward way of living and minimal social and economic mobility. Regardless, the Maxwell Street marketplace became a focal point of the community. It was an open-market bazaar and the site of diverse peddlers and merchandise. There were kosher meat markets, matzoh bakeries, dry goods stores, peddlers' stables that sold fruit and vegetables, tailor and seamstress shops and more.[51] Though this colorful marketplace made sense to the Russian Jews, outsiders did not understand its appeal and focused on its poor condition. For example, in the same July 1891 article, the *Chicago Tribune* notes, "A venture into a rag warehouse to one not used to the atmosphere is nearly fatal."[52]

Of course, there were some who moved out as soon as they could create the opportunity, but as a whole, the Russian Jews might not have minded the limitations of the ghetto. After all, they had escaped the May Laws and the pogroms of the old country. Furthermore, they were able to transplant the character of the revered shtetl culture into the near West Side—manifest in the Orthodox lifestyle and Maxwell Street market. However, the same could not always be said of their children—the gangster generation.

There was, in fact, a growing distance between the immigrant and American-born generations. The *Chicago Tribune* took notice of this gap on July 19, 1891: "The younger generation of men are more progressive and, having been born in this country, are patriotic and want to be known as Americans and not Russians."[53] Yet its explanation ran deeper than want of patriotism. Philip P. Bregstone, a contemporary Chicago Jew, provides a more complete justification. "The Jewish Child," he wrote, "could not fathom [his parents'] inner selves, steeped as they were in old world heritages and beliefs, and was unable to comprehend their outer life."[54] This increasing estrangement of children from their immigrant parents is a largely unspoken aspect of Chicago Jewish history but vital to understanding part of the reason why some Jewish children grew into crime. Bregstone continues, "It was not strange that the Jewish children of immigrant parents contributed in a large measure to child delinquency."[55] It would seem, then, that early Jewish crime was in part the reaction of a younger generation to all that their parents worked hard to preserve—religious Orthodoxy and the Old World lifestyle—and provided the children with an escape.

Yet on the contrary, crime was sometimes a child's way of coping with his parents' absence and neglect. This was perhaps a consequence of unsuccessfully transitioning to American life, succumbing to the extraordinary pressures of making ends meet or simply living in a dysfunctional environment. Case 31 of the Chicago Committee on Crime's investigation of children at the State Reformatory for Boys at St. Charles, published in 1915, was one such example. The subject was a seven-year-old Jewish boy from Russia at the time of his file's opening in January 1906. The Child Study Department of the Public Schools (CSD) noted that it was "wholly a case of poor home conditions."[56] The succinct entries of the CSD, the Juvenile Psychopathic Institute (JPI) and others, spanning an eight-year period, chronicled a lamentable story of a boy with no familial support who wandered the streets for weeks at a time, shuffled from orphanage homes to institutes and always ran away. On September 11, 1911, the JPI observed that he was "very defective in self-control on the basis of defective heredity" and indicated, "Parent insane. Father unknown."[57] Thus the JPI linked the boy's deviant behavior directly to his parents. In October 1912, the court charged the boy with criminal assault of a three-year-old girl after he had fled from his mother for New York. Two years later, in the report's final entry, St. Charles Reformatory resolutely believed the child to be recidivistic and unlikely to function in society. His case illuminates a childhood experience not unique among Chicago immigrant families—Jewish or gentile. However much the children attempted to escape the ways of their parents, they did require a nurturing environment facilitated by parental care and guidance.

Furthermore, there were other factors beyond childhood rebellion and lack of parental care that gave rise to the gangster generation. I contend that an inadequate system of education and a hunger for greater social mobility also made a turn to the streets increasingly attractive. As a whole, Jewish educators faced several challenges in developing a school system for their respective American communities. All the problems revolved around striking a balance between individuality and assimilation. They needed a system that would transmit a sufficient cultural identity without segregating their children from the rest of American life. Additionally, the Jewish educators needed to consider "how to help the Jewish individual adjust himself to the American environment without adjusting himself out of his Jewish group."[58] Moreover, the deep cleavage between the German and the Russian Jews compounded the difficulties. The contrast between ideologies of Reform and Orthodox Judaism meant differences not only in social position, outlook and wealth, but also in religious values.[59] In fact, a poor system of education did not affect the children of the German immigrants as profoundly as those of the Russian Jews. The Germans were better assimilated into mainstream society, in part because of the Reform Judaism they adopted, and many had been successful businessmen since the nineteenth century, which allowed for more economic mobility than among the Russians. Evident, then, is the interconnectedness of all these differences that developed between the German and Russian Jews. The specifics of the education system that did eventually develop are outside the boundaries of this study.[60]

However, it is important to note that the difficulties outlined above resulted in a generation born in limbo. The Jewish children had neither deep roots in the New World nor the Old. They were bereft of an appreciation for Jewish values and tradition, and consequently, the educational standards of the gangster generation were extraordinarily low.[61] Without the guidance that parents and school typically afford, juvenile delinquency seems almost an obvious product in the Jewish community on the near West Side. This disillusionment experienced by the second generation of Jewish immigrants was not unique to this group alone. Historian Marcus Lee Hansen noted a general phenomenon that occurred among children of all American immigrants in his speech, "The Problem of the Third Generation Immigrant."[62] Hansen argued that the children of immigrants were on the receiving end of criticism and mockery from both their parents and established Americans—the former making even life at home unpleasant. He declared, "How to inhabit two worlds at the same time was the problem of the second generation."[63] Often, the solution to this problem was escape. Hansen maintained that the immigrant child wanted to forget everything he knew—his foreign language, religion and customs.[64]

Indeed, the younger generation's hunger for greater social mobility also added to the allure of delinquency and crime at the turn of the century. It is clear that the realities of the ghetto severely limited the economic opportunities for Jews living there. Sociologist James O'Kane asserts that all ethnic minorities utilize seven routes to secure social mobility, and he further distinguishes between legitimate, semi-legitimate and illegitimate avenues. O'Kane suggests that the legitimate routes include unskilled and semiskilled labor, retail small business, the professions, the clergy and the entertainment business. Sometimes, however, ethnic minorities will achieve social mobility through urban politics (a semi-legitimate route) and crime (an illegitimate avenue).[65] Following this model, it appears that most of the Chicago Jewry used legitimate routes. Yet the Jews of the gangster generation, perhaps after witnessing their parents' fruitless toil, became frustrated and impatient with the reputable methods of climbing the ethnic ladder. Additionally, the nature of the ghetto might have overwhelmed some of the youth, leaving an impressionable mark of the exact life not to lead.

Similarly, historian Mark H. Haller demonstrates the importance of the Chicago underworld in offering social mobility to immigrants who might not have found it elsewhere. It is important to note that his explanations, like that of O'Kane, apply to second-generation ethnic groups in general, not just to Jews. Haller identifies three occupational paths young persons of an ethnic community could pursue. The groups broadly comprise the poor working class, the educated professionals and governmental employees and the occupations "open to uneducated and ambitious ethnic youths."[66] This last group includes crime, participation in local machine politics, sports, entertainment and leadership in Chicago's labor unions.[67] Subsequent examples of Chicago Jewry's criminal involvement will serve to illuminate the inherent connection between crime and social mobility that these two scholars helped to establish.

By the turn of the century, the stage was set for children of the Eastern European immigrants to disproportionately turn to the city's streets and underworld. In the early decades of the twentieth century, youth street gangs constructed, defended and reinforced racial and ethnic identities along community boundaries. Interactions between youth subcultures of Irish

On a sidewalk with pots of food for the Sabbath, Jewish men and boys stand, Chicago, 1903. *Chicago History Museum, DN-0001468, Chicago Daily News, Inc.*

and Poles, Jews and Poles and Poles and Italians reified "cultures of racial hostility."[68] Sociologist Frederic Thrasher placed the ghetto within what he called the "West Side Wilderness"—the most expansive gangland domain in Chicago.[69] Here were gangs of Poles that proliferated along Milwaukee Avenue, groups of Irish youth, Italian boys, African Americans known as the "Coons from Lake Street" and Jewish gangs.[70] Moreover, Jewish youth crime would eventually continue beyond the "Wilderness" and the ghetto into areas of second settlement, such as the middle-class Jewish community of Lawndale. These areas, too, will be important to keep in mind, realizing that many Jews were not confined to the ghetto their entire lives.

By 1900, though the initial composition of the community was set, Chicago Jewish crime—both disorganized and organized—would prove to play a significant role in shaping the life of the Jewish community. It would force the community members to make sense of and respond to the wrongdoings and criminal behaviors in relation to the current value sets emphasized in their religion, culture and family life. Crime is an often forgotten aspect in the history of the Chicago Jewry. Cutler, Wirth and Meites—the Jewish scholars who laid the groundwork for this chapter—mention it only fleetingly. Whether it has been deliberately forgotten and suppressed for the sake of Jewish pride or simply overlooked, it is time to realize the full significance of crime.

2

ETHNIC RELATIONS, BOYS' GANGS AND COMMUNITY CONCERN

1900–1925

Life in glass windows was a great deal safer.[71]
—*Abraham Bisno, intimating the dangers of life in the streets at the turn of the century*

In the summer of 1900, Chairman Robert Hunter and the executive committee of the City Homes Association set out to write an assessment of the tenement conditions in Chicago. They selected several districts for analysis, including the Polish community in the Sixteenth Ward and the Italian district in the Nineteenth Ward, in addition to the West Side Jewish ghetto. What they found in these areas was dismal. Among the crowded tenements and dangerous, ill-paved sidewalks, the committee noticed a complete absence of playgrounds. Hunter reported, "In the failure to satisfy this need of the children [the universal necessity for play and imagination] with properly equipped municipal playgrounds the street habit and the gang habit become the causes of a large percentage of juvenile crime."[72] The "street habit" was the children's use of these open spaces as a substitute for playgrounds. Though Hunter did not define the "gang habit," he was alluding to the need for children to belong and their tendency to congregate in and form groups. Hilda Satt Polacheck, a Jew from Poland who arrived in the city as a child in 1892, grew up in the ghetto on South Halsted Street—four blocks south of Jane Addams's Hull-House. She remembered, "The only play space was the street in front of the house," and "there was not a tree or a blade of grass anywhere in the neighborhood."[73]

Both testimonies signify that a child living in the ghetto or other equally bleak districts at the turn of the century looked to the streets for an escape from the crowded residences and for fulfillment of childhood recreation and exploration normally realized on the playgrounds. However, this recreation was liable to turn errant, resulting in disorganized youth crime—that of boys' gangs and adolescent street gangs at or below the age of twenty-one. Disorganized and organized crimes are not mutually exclusive but rather part of a continuum with blurry boundaries separating the two. Nonetheless, the former must be understood in order to grasp the latter. It is on the streets where the youths distanced themselves from their parents and where the older and younger generations of Jews confronted the ills they thought they had left behind in the Old World. With the inadequacies of the municipality, the streets exposed the Jewish community and its youth to the continued realities of anti-Semitism, fostered interactions with other ethnic groups and proliferated the involvement of Jews in boys' gangs—creating a synergy among the three that produced an array of opinions and actions from the Jewish community at large.

I

Attacks on Jewish street peddlers and merchants were an early manifestation of the hostility against Chicago's Jews. The lively Maxwell Street market was the hotspot for several instances of this "Jew baiting" because, along with small business operations, many Jews made their livings as small merchants on the streets.[74] The problem was widespread, causing alarm not only in the Jewish community but also in the city as a whole. On March 25, 1901, the *Chicago Tribune* positioned "Jews Organize to Resist Attacks" as the day's third leading story.[75] That same day, an article entitled "Woes of the Peddlers: Jewish Merchants Hold an Indignation Meeting" made the edition's first page, effectively demonstrating the attention the problem of Jew baiting had garnered, its severity and the community's response.

At West Thirteenth and Jefferson Streets, one hundred Jewish peddlers and some prominent non-Jewish figures, such as Clarence Darrow and Jane Addams, piled into Rochester Hall to voice their concerns and to demand greater police protection for the Jews. They proclaimed that hoodlums assault twelve men in Chicago daily for the sole reason that the victims are Jews. The following testimony from H. Goldberg, a Jew and former street

A man of the Maxwell Street market, Chicago, circa 1917. *Chicago History Museum, DN-0068690, Chicago Daily News, Inc.*

peddler, epitomized the meeting's sentiment. He declared, "We are stoned by boys and assaulted by hoodlums wherever we go, and the police stand by and laugh. We are called 'sheeney' and abused on every hand, but the authorities make no effort to protect us. The Jewish people are peaceable

Portrait of an older man holding lemons at the Maxwell Street market, Chicago, circa 1910–29. *Chicago History Museum, ICHi-65376, Jun Fujita.*

and law-abiding. The Italian and Greek peddlers are not attacked because the boys know that they carry knives and will fight back."[76] Goldberg's account illustrated the rampancy of anti-Semitic attacks on the streets, which reached beyond the ghetto's boundaries and frightened the immigrants who believed they had left such prejudice behind in the Old World. Additionally, his testimony introduced a common theme—the Jewish community's perception of its members as upstanding and virtuous citizens—which was constantly challenged in the twentieth century. However, the policemen's ostensible approval of the assaults and the city's failure to enforce the law was even more startling. In turn, after several Jewish speakers spoke in anger and echoed Goldberg's reflections, the members of the meeting resolved to form the Chicago Protective League and designated a committee of Jewish men to handle its organization with the hopes of ensuring greater police protection in the future.

Though the meeting represented a concerted effort by the Jewish community to halt Jew baiting and demand more police support, the problems persisted. Nearly five years after the formation of the Chicago Protective League, in February 1906, the *Chicago Tribune* ran another article appealing to the policemen to stop teenage hoodlums from committing wrongdoings against "inoffensive" Jewish peddlers.[77] This particular incident occurred at the corner of Polk and Morgan Streets, approximately four blocks north of the Maxwell Street market. The article stated that the young transgressors were part of a neighborhood gang and that the "spirit of hoodlumism [had] pervaded the district," where Jews were often its victims.[78] As before, the report charged the policemen with the responsibility to quell the Jew baiting, but unlike the 1901 article, this one placed emphasis on the profile of the offenders. It demonstrates the existence of juvenile delinquency and the mixing of the various ethnic community members on the ghetto streets, which will become more pronounced in subsequent pages. In November of the same year, hundreds of irate Jews, residing in the ghetto district, convened in the West Side auditorium, determined to protect their old and defenseless co-religionists from the boys' gangs. The products of this meeting were the Chicago Jewish Protective Association and the notion that the parents of these hoodlums were responsible for watching their children, not the police.[79]

To no avail—problems of Jew baiting and Anti-Semitism would persist in Chicago and across America throughout this period. In 1908, Dr. Emil Hirsch, a nationally known rabbi of the Sinai Congregation in Chicago, declared, "It is an offensive social prejudice against the Jew [anti-Semitism] wherein America at the present moment outstrips the world."[80] This was a bold statement considering the high degree of discrimination Jews had experienced in their homelands. Yet ethnic enmities between the Jews and both the Irish and Polish communities in Chicago were exceptionally contentious. Analyzing each of these controversial relationships individually is vital because the interactions would often translate into the dynamics seen in the city's underworld, among the youth and adult gangsters.

As early as the 1880s, there were signs of friction between the Jewish and Irish communities of Chicago. The Irish were not necessarily wealthier than the Jews, but they had arrived to the city first. In turn, they perhaps felt that the Jews had encroached on their territory and were thus entitled to intimidate the new immigrants. Abraham Bisno, a Jewish immigrant from Russia and future labor leader of Chicago Jewish garment workers, grew up on Canal and Twelfth Streets in the late nineteenth century. He recalled the inhospitality of the adjacent Irish neighborhood. Jews with whiskers "were stoned [by the Irish]; in winter snowballs were thrown at them; and some of the street bums would run by, pull their beards, and beat them." He also observed, "I remember innumerable fights in the ghetto streets between Irish rowdies and our own rowdies," and during social gatherings, their resentment for the Irish increasingly became the topic of conversation.[81] Of course, it is never fair to speak in absolutes, but there were several instances in the first twenty-five years of the twentieth century in which Irishmen, typically characterized as drunkards or hoodlums, attacked Jews.

The Yiddish press took notice. In November 1913, the *Daily Jewish Courier*, the Yiddish voice of Chicago Orthodox Jewry, reported that the Valley gang, a seasoned Irish street gang, had attacked the Jewish district yet again. The writer's use of "again" signifies that this clearly was not an isolated incident by the Valley gang but part of an established problem. On this occasion, the group of drunken gangsters rode into the area in an automobile and pummeled forty-year-old Louis Switzky, a Jew.[82] The gang's joy rides, although recurrent, appeared to be for the pleasure and amusement of its members and rather sporadic. Yet this was not always the case. In 1916, Irish ruffians instigated a larger attack against the Jewish community near Taylor and Cypress Streets, leaving eighteen Jews injured and the neighborhood "like the aftermath of a battle."[83] Curiously, the *Daily Jewish Courier* reported that it was in fact a premeditated attack, but when the "peaceful Jewish residents" requested police protection, the Thirteenth Street Police Station allegedly ignored the plea. This speaks either to the Irishmen's great influence in the district or to the spill of anti-Semitism into every avenue of the city, or to both.

Contrasting the territorialism of the Irish, the Polish community's enmity toward the Jews was deeper-seated. The Poles transplanted the intercultural hostilities of the Old World to Chicago, and thus, it greatly intensified "during periods when the Jews in anti-Semitic countries are suffering from pogroms."[84] It is no surprise, then, that the summer of 1919 serves as a paradigm for the two groups' antagonistic relationship. On May 23, along the streets of Moscow, Russia, one could hear the angry mob shout, "Down with the Jews!"[85] In Poland, 54 Jews succumbed to pogroms throughout April and May, often instigated by the Polish government itself.[86] Back in Chicago a few weeks thereafter, the Chicago Poles attempted to stage a pogrom of their own in the Douglas Park district. Yet the Poles never showed up to the park, in part due to the 250 extra policemen deployed, but also because of tough Jewish boys—"unarmed but ready to fight with sinewy muscles to defend the Jewish population from those who sought Jewish blood."[87] This outcome frustrated park police, said to be 80 percent Polish, who had previously facilitated assaults by Poles on the Jews within the park's confines. The thwarted pogrom, of course, elated the Jews. The *Daily Jewish Courier* interviewed Davey Miller in his popular lunchroom at 3216 West Twelfth Street to get his reactions. We will see that he and his brothers were major Jewish figures in the Chicago underworld and that Davey was often candid with the media. Davey proudly told the reporter, "I am more of a Jewish Jew than they think I am…if it were not for me and all the boys that come here, Jews would be murdered in this neighborhood. We have eliminated the petty thieves, and hope in the future, to continue to live in peace and safety."[88] Miller's ties to Judaism and perceived role as protector of the community are equally intriguing. Moreover, the statement illuminates the importance of the Jewish gangsters in diffusing intercultural hostilities.[89]

Not all of the confrontations between Jews and Poles were pogroms. For example, on June 18, 1919, the *Daily Jewish Courier* covered the attack on Jewish junk dealer B. Tshertcof by twenty Polish hoodlums. This incident, which involved the stoning of Mr. Tshertcof, more closely resembled the Irish delinquents' antics. In fact, sometimes these two ethnic groups collaborated against the Jews. In 1924, a group of Irish and Polish bums near Stanford Park, who had previously only heckled Jewish youth walking by, began to batter the Jewish boys seeking leisure at the play area or nearby library. One victim, Max Kustiner, could barely reach his home at 560 West Twelfth Place following the altercation due to his injuries.[90] Understanding the Jews' intercultural enmities with the Irish and Poles helps to make sense of why Jewish gangsters oftentimes associated themselves with certain criminals or gangs while avoiding others.

However, the Jewish community had more to fear than simply guarding against anti-Semitic attacks. They also became concerned with what was happening in their community internally, particularly among the youth, who bound together in gangs in the face of this discrimination.

II

Though published in 1927, Frederic Thrasher's *The Gang: A Study of 1,313 Gangs in Chicago* is an extraordinary analysis for understanding the ins and outs of juvenile delinquency and street gangs in the early twentieth century. He began collecting data for this extensive book in 1920, and since he relied heavily on the memories of the youth he interviewed, his findings trace back even earlier and are pertinent to this study. According to Thrasher, Chicago street gangs were often the products of poor immigrant communities.[91] Childhood gangs consisted of children, typically ages six to twelve, who were mischievous, closely affiliated with the "play-group" and diffuse in their organization. They congregated in all the open spaces of the neighborhood.[92] Though the ghetto began without a park area, as Hilda Polacheck and Chairman Hunter described, the West Park commissioners purchased property for "breathing spots" in 1908. Bohemian, Jewish, Irish and Polish dwellings densely surrounded the future park, bounded by Fourteenth Place and Barber, Jefferson and Union Streets.[93] Places like these, as well as the open area of the Maxwell Street market, educated the children in areas beyond arithmetic and reading comprehension. It taught the children street smarts—i.e., how to function without parental supervision and to behave when among peers of similar or contrasting backgrounds. The street and such forms of informal education were "far more vital in the life of the child than the conventional types" and important to keep in mind.[94]

As the boy reached his teenage years, leaving his childhood gang behind, he might have joined an adolescent gang. They were better organized than the younger boys, normally unsupervised and thus more likely to get into trouble. Moreover, they generally had specific hangouts, such as a particular street corner or barn.[95] Though these street gangs might appear to be innocent cases of boys fraternizing with one another, the consequences were sometimes quite severe. Take, for example, Walsh Elementary School, located four blocks south of the Jewish ghetto. According to a 1906 *Chicago Tribune* article, it was the longstanding site of a race war among the ghetto boys and those from surrounding neighborhoods.[96] On March 4, a pupil shot and killed Stanley Zavadil, twelve years old, at the school as a result of a skirmish between two rival factions. Two months prior, police had arrested Zavadil for possession of a revolver, and he subsequently told the judge he felt compelled to carry the weapon in self-defense.[97] A later article revealed that Arthur Heler, one of Zavadil's friends, was the culprit and that the shooting was accidental. Apparently, it happened while the children were attacking a group of Jewish boys. An article from the *Chicago Tribune* declared, "There are gangs whose purpose it is to annoy the Jew boys, gangs whose object is to get even with the Italians, and other gangs whose sole endeavor seems to be to flourish weapons and fight their youthful comrades."[98] This instance verifies the seriousness of the boys' gang problem and the degree of ethnic interactions their activities fostered in public areas. It did not go unnoticed within the Jewish community.

On November 6, 1913, E.M. Wolfson wrote a sizeable editorial in the *Daily Jewish Courier* entitled "The Young Gangster in Chicago." Wolfson wanted the Jewish community to reflect on comments made by a reporter from a large English-speaking newspaper in Chicago concerning the problem of street gangs. This columnist studied boys' gangs extensively, and much of what Wolfson included from the writer mirrored Thrasher's remarks concerning the progression from childhood to adolescent gangs. What might have begun as a club with good intentions of play and recreation sometimes turned into a group of delinquents with little direction. However, Wolfson demonstrated that the author placed particular emphasis on the responsibility of the parents and the community: "The remarkable feature in this gang situation is that most parents of these children know about them but take very little interest in the matter. These parents generally give one of two excuses: They believe it is an innocent club for boys that their son belongs to, or, on the other hand if they know the nature of the gang they have no knowledge of their boy's being a member there."[99] Rather than relying on the police force to halt these young gangsters, the editorial pushed for greater parental oversight and care with an entire community invested in the troubles of delinquency. Yet there is an even more fascinating aspect of E.M. Wolfson's editorial. It is evident that he was appealing to the Jewish community, perhaps specifically to the ghetto, since Yiddish is a language for the Orthodox Jews. However, he did so without condemning the Jewish youth in particular or even acknowledging that the problem was in existence right underneath their noses. It simply introduced his readership to the growing problem of the city.

Nevertheless, street gangs were prevalent among the Jewish youth. In *The Gang*, Thrasher confirmed the race and nationalities of 880 gangs and cited 20 of these as Jewish groups. Yet this number is misleadingly small, as the number of mixed nationality gangs was 351—nearly 40 percent of all the gangs. Comparatively, the Jewish youth furnished the fourth greatest number of homogenous gangs, behind the Polish, Italian and Irish, who had 148, 99 and 75 gangs, respectively.[100] Thrasher attributed this discrepancy in gang totals to several factors. The Jewish youth, in elementary as well as high schools, tended to band together in order to resist discrimination, which is why understanding the heavy presence of anti-Semitism in and around the Jewish community is critical.[101] In turn, they typically formed under conditions of severe duress, as was often the case with the opposition from their Polish neighbors.[102] Due in part to the religiosity stressed by their parents, Jewish, Polish and Irish children likely had an equally organized family and leisure lifestyle. This would seemingly deter a child from turning to the streets for amusement and exploration; however, it was often the Polish and Irish devoutness that contributed to anti-Semitism. Moreover, Thrasher stated that the "individualistic spirit of the Jews" accounted for the smaller number of gangs, but I do not believe this to be true. Nearly all activities, religious and otherwise, emphasized familial and communal participation and were above all else social gatherings. Consequently, Jewish boys, like all others, would seek fraternization, especially if it meant protection.[103]

The Jewish gangs that flourished in the ghetto district, such as the old "Boundary Gang," were collectively known as the "Jews from Twelfth Street" and intermittently engaged in fights with groups from neighboring regions.[104] During one of Thrasher's interviews, a gang boy recalled, "We fought the Jews from Twelfth Street, but they had too many for us. They're pretty good fighters. We knew they had more than we did, so we went down with clubs and everything."[105] As evidenced by this testimony, the Jewish gangsters did fight, though they were often thought of as more cerebral than physical beings. Additionally, it appeared that the Jewish boys' gangs had a proclivity toward a certain criminal activity—pickpocketing—which the crowded Maxwell Street market facilitated. Sociologist John Landesco, who grew up an immigrant on Chicago's West Side, told of the relationship between Jews and the pickpocket occupation in Chicago. His profiling of the Chicago pickpockets was succinct: "They are immigrants from Russia and New York, and nearly all of them are Jews. Chicago pickpockets are overwhelmingly from the Ghetto."[106] This testimony reinforces my contention that the majority of Chicago's Jewish criminals were Eastern Europeans who settled in the ghetto and not German immigrants. A brief 1914 *Daily Jewish Courier* article confirms Landesco's description. It spoke of Jewish second-class detective Sergeant Michael Weisbaum, of the Maxwell Street Police Station—located in the ghetto's center—and his recent successes and continual efforts to purge the West Side of its pickpockets.[107] Chicago's chief of police James Gleason praised Weisbaum for his work. While a 1914 *Chicago Tribune* report wrote on the secret investigation by

Chicago's crime commission, which exposed the connection between West Side pickpockets and paid police protection, its findings applied only to the older pickpockets.[108] The above *Daily Jewish Courier* article gives credence to this notion, as does the reality of boys' gangs often avoiding and hiding from district police officers.

It is true that gangs from other regions took advantage of the congested atmosphere that was the Maxwell Street market for thieving, but none more than Itschkie's Black Hand Society, a Jewish pickpocket gang.[109]

An intimate observer of the gang, along with various interviews and records, compose the manuscript included in Frederic Thrasher's *The Gang*. There is little known about this Jewish boys' gang aside from this account, perhaps because of its name, incidentally the same as the one applied to Italian-American extortionist groups found across American cities during the same period.[110] However, the common name is not so coincidental after learning the composition of Itschkie's Black Hand Society. Approximately fifteen boys, aged twelve to fifteen years old, composed the gang. Its members

Men standing by street vending booths at the Maxwell Street market, Chicago, 1922. *Chicago History Museum, DN-0075248, Chicago Daily News, Inc.*

An elevated view of the Maxwell Street market, illustrating the crowds that gathered, Chicago, 1917. *Chicago History Museum, DN-0068691, Chicago Daily News, Inc.*

resided primarily in the Maxwell Street neighborhood. Interestingly, all were Jewish save two Italian juveniles. According to the manuscript, the Jews admitted the "Greasers...because of their compatibility and their residence in the neighborhood."[111] The process of admittance described by the observer was rather extensive.[112] In turn, the gang's borrowed name and the mix of Jewish and Italian members speak volumes of the amicable relationship between these two ethnic communities. This is especially true when contrasted with the often-contentious relationship between the Jews and both the Irish and Poles. Indeed, the marrying of Jews and Italians in gangs would spill over into the more organized crime outfits, such as the Syndicate, where Al Capone befriended a Jew who would become a surprisingly close confidant.

Yet the Black Hand Society was not the ordinary adolescent gang. They did have the characteristic designated hangout; theirs was in an abandoned house, known as the "Roamer's Inn," where the boys hid from police and partook in various forms of vice, like shooting craps.[113] However, these Jews and "Greasers" had more structure and success than most at their age. Itschkie's method of picking a pocket involved the entire gang, dividing the boys into groups of three to four with each faction playing a unique part in the operation. When the boys wanted quicker money and some fun, they would target drunken men and blind beggars in a less involved process. On a given Sunday, their ringleader, Itschkie, could earn twenty-five to thirty dollars and once made off with eighty dollars from such robberies. Silver, one of Thrasher's interviewees and a youth gangster on good terms with the Black Handers, noted a striking feature of these activities: "They hop the poor drunken Polish fellows. They respect the Jews more because they are most all Jews themselves."[114] Delinquent as they were, then, the boys did seem to value and positively identify with their fellow Jews, perhaps not wanting to inhibit the success of the larger Jewish community.

Consequently, while the manuscript suggested that the primary motive behind the Black Hand Society's operations was excitement, it was more likely a means for the boys to find their place in society and to secure some cash.[115] Though not born out of self-protection, as Jewish street gangs often were, the Black Handers' solidarity and socialization aided to ease the growing estrangement from their Orthodox parents and anti-Semitism, which augmented feelings of isolation normally experienced by teenagers. Additionally, if the members' families had been well off, they would have likely moved out of the ghetto district and into a more comfortable area of second settlement. In turn, the fact that these boys still lived in ghetto residences reveals much of their families' meager economic situations. What boy would then deny the chance to earn twenty-five to thirty dollars in a single day when money was hard to gain? Excitement and amusement were certainly part of the equation, but so were economic mobility and fraternization.

As some Jewish families prospered—perhaps succeeding in small business ventures, gaining access to marginal social and economic mobility—segments of the community migrated northward and westward out of the ghetto to areas of second settlement, such as Lawndale.[116] This movement was manifest in the establishment of new institutions critical to the Jewish community. In July 1917, over 10,000 Jews celebrated the opening of a new Jewish center and Talmud Torah in the Lawndale district.[117] Yet the newfound social mobility and institutions did not equate to an end to juvenile delinquency. In actuality, Lawndale, as well as the communities on the Northwest Side, had difficulties keeping up with the population explosion. The *Chicago Hebrew*

Institute Observer, the monthly newsletter of the vital community center in the Maxwell Street area, alone voiced its concerns of the burgeoning Lawndale district. By January 1919, the publication estimated the population of Lawndale at nearly 100,000 Jews.[118] It charged the nearsighted district with not providing adequate means of self-expression for the children, in turn putting young men and women in the position to find avenues of recreation and sociality in the darkest of places. Consequently, the newsletter lamented, "in the Juvenile Court, the Boys' Court…of which formerly it was the Jew's pride to be able to state that so far as he was concerned, they need not exist, he now has to bow his head in shame when he visits them, for in their daily dockets he hears the names of the Goldsteins and the Bernsteins called much oftener than is necessary."[119] It intimates the regret with which some of the older Jews spoke of their dissident sons and daughters. Clearly, it was an affront to their pride, integral to the solidarity of the Jewish people, and their shaming of the youth's involvement was a common reaction among the community. Moreover, though the article might have been a ploy to create a new branch of the Chicago Hebrew Institute in Lawndale, it demonstrates, nonetheless, that the problem of juvenile delinquency persisted in areas of second settlement into the 1920s.

Additionally, the migrations forged new Jewish-Polish frontiers, in places like Humboldt Park, Lawndale and nearby Douglas Park, that became central to the intercultural fights discussed earlier. According to a resident close to Douglas Park, there were various assaults on Jewish boys by hoodlums of the Polish community to the southeast in the summer of 1921. To return the favor, a gang of young Jews, led by Samuel "Nails" Morton— later an organized crime figure—left their poolroom hangouts to "Wallop the Polock."[120] That the Jews typically did not know the Poles personally was irrelevant. "It was a matter of racial, cultural and religious solidarity," as past instances had certainly demonstrated.[121]

III

The Jewish community did not simply accept their youths' stray from Orthodoxy, wild behavior and involvement in boys' gangs. Rather, they attempted to make sense of the recent changes. Since there is little testimony available from the community members, I rely primarily on the Yiddish newspapers to gain insight into their reactions for two reasons.

First, the Yiddish press was highly influential and the voice of the Jewish community, with nearly all literate Chicago Jews regularly reading the papers. Second, well-regarded members of the community, including various rabbis, school principals and scholars, wrote several of the articles, which suggests that, overall, their opinions would have been equally respected by the Jewish readership. The juvenile delinquency precipitated an array of responses and methodological approaches to solving the problem through the first twenty-five years of the century. However, the authors commonly emphasized sentiments of shame and disbelief, the victimization of their children and the desire for a return to former times. Furthermore, the various courses of action they recommended included parental, educational and institutional reform.

Jews were a self-conscious people. With all the anti-Semitic fervor in the Old and New Worlds alike, it is no wonder that the gentile community's perception of their people weighed heavily on the Jews' minds. It was no different for the Jews of Chicago. In some ways, acceptance was their most basic desire. This certainly explains why, beginning in the late 1880s, the influx of poor Russian Jews and subsequent formation of the ghetto troubled the German Jews, who were unsure of how it would affect the city's perception of their people.[122] These same concerns confronted the Jewish community when their youth increasingly turned to the streets and joined boys' gangs. Initially, many Jews were impoverished and were already experiencing a high degree of hostility from their ethnic neighbors. As a result, they believed the delinquency further delayed the day when the gentile community of Chicago would perceive the Jews as a respectable and dignified people. An anonymous 1912 editorial in the *Jewish Daily Courier* reflected these sentiments in relation to the rise of gun use among the youth: "Every honest and loyal Jew would rather see the past when a Jew feared a gun than the present when Jewish children use guns as toys and cause death and corruption. The heroism—not fearing death—is not a phenomenon of courage, but of arrogance and dissoluteness."[123] Two years later, the *Courier* pleaded to the community, "Help eradicate this shame from the Jewish district. Do it for your children's sake so that they might not become victims of this plague."[124] Both articles denounced the delinquency of the youth, but it is curious that the latter referred to the children as victims. This signifies a certain distancing from the crime and vice—a way to hold society responsible for the phenomenon and not its children. Moreover, it displaces the blame from the Jewish community, perhaps in an attempt to maintain their dignity.

Amid the community's anger and shame, echoed in the words of the Yiddish press, were various suggestions of how to rid the youth of crime. One such approach was parent-oriented. These people believed that the key to a child's success was a moral upbringing under the direction of his parents. Above all, it was up to the parents to prevent their malleable children from deviance on the streets. An example of this method appeared in the *Chicago Chronicle* in 1924. "Every person at some period in his youth passes through a difficult time…The parents of the least extraordinary of children will do well to watch for this critical time, to provide against it, to build up self-respect and respect for others, and above all, not leave the youngster too much to his own devices."[125] It was no coincidence that the writer penned the column in July because the crowded and sweltering conditions of the tenements often forced children onto the streets during the summer.[126] Moreover, it was in the summertime that children had the most time for leisure and thus the greatest opportunity to stray from a moral path. Additionally, the emphasis was on parental supervision and ethical education at home. An advantage to this approach was that the newspaper could directly reach and speak to its intended audience—the parents—but its successes were hard to measure because the changes occurred inside the home.

No Jew denied the importance of a parent's presence in molding, both positively and negatively, the life of a child. However, some believed that the principal answer to keeping the youth off the streets was a greater religious education. According to sociologist Louis Wirth, a family's status within the Jewish community depended chiefly on the learning of their children, so the concern was not only for the youngster but also for the parents' social standing.[127] Utilizing the *Daily Jewish Courier* as his medium, Moses Levin, principal of a Talmud Torah, contended that the more children who receive a religious education, the fewer the number of Jewish children in the juvenile court records.[128] While parents were off struggling to make ends meet, Levin maintained that the Jewish teacher would fulfill the father's role of guardian, authority and friend to the "living orphan." Additionally, he believed the Jewish and moral education would keep the child occupied, effectively keeping him off the streets. He concluded, "If a few Jewish children are sent to Pontiac [correctional center], then we begin a rumpus by crying that the Jewish name is being ridiculed and disgraced," and he begged the entire Chicago Jewish community to push for an expansion of the Jewish school system.[129]

Levin was not alone in his convictions. In truth, several writers analyzed the relationship between juvenile crime and low levels of Judaism in their articles. One Jewish journalist remarked that a departure from the Torah and the basic tenements of Judaism was to blame for the new generation of Americanized Jewish criminals. He believed that in order to right the wrong, the Jewish youth had to acquaint themselves with the words of their forgotten prophets.[130] The author of "For the Benefit of Small Children," a *Daily Jewish Courier* article from May 1, 1917, further explored the absence of Jewish studies in the lives of the youth. At the time of the report, of the approximately 48,000 Jewish children in the city, 40,000 attended Chicago public schools, while only 8,000 studied in Jewish schools. The repercussions were clear to the author: "The children despise their parents, whose conduct and ideals are foreign to them…they are turning away from their religion…and they violate the laws of social morals."[131] Further, the author proclaimed that 98 percent of the 350 Jewish boys admitted to the Juvenile Detention Home had never attended a Hebrew school. Whether this statistic is accurate is beside the point. The author used it to connect Judaism to morality. His proposed solution had several components but essentially argued for more modern schools that offered Jewish studies on the West Side and a concrete plan to educate Jewish sons and daughters to teach at these schools. The American-born teachers, though having good intentions, were not cutting it. Yet another *Daily Jewish Courier* article stressed how school had the power to provide the child with a balanced, stimulated environment that would surround him with the positive influences necessary to keep him out of trouble, including many athletic groups and school clubs. Moreover, the teacher had the ability to bring school and home closer together, leaving the streets out of the equation.[132]

Beyond the desire to reestablish and strengthen Judaic studies in the lives of their youth, members of the Jewish community also believed in institutional reform to correct the problem of juvenile delinquency. The Chicago Hebrew Institute (CHI) in the Maxwell Street area was one such example. CHI strove to Americanize its immigrants while still maintaining Jewish traditions. The institute offered an assortment of educational, recreational and social programs for young and old alike, in addition to having a library, synagogue, playgrounds and even a gymnasium.[133] However vital to the community, CHI managed to face a fiscal deficit in 1914 due to low membership levels. In turn, an appeal for new members was the aim of the 1914 *Daily Jewish Courier* editorial. In order to secure greater support, the column related the CHI's success in protecting the youth from the city's vices. For the children who regularly participated in the institute's activities, the advocate affirmed there would be no use for any of the evils, like pickpocketing or gambling, "with which the newspapers are replete with Jewish names of people who did not share the good fortune of having a Chicago Hebrew Institute, when they first came here."[134] To these supporters, the CHI provided the children with a religious education, moral direction and a stimulated environment—effectively coupling several of the parental- and educational-based goals.

Institutional advocacy seemed to apply particularly to those concerned with the burgeoning Lawndale district. Jewish judge Harry M. Fisher, of the city's Boys' Court, agreed with the merit of the CHI—renamed to the Jewish People's Institute (JPI) in the early 1920s. Speaking to the Jewish community, he pledged, "A branch of the Jewish People's Institute, in the Lawndale district will...keep the Jewish youth out of the poolrooms and other nests of crime."[135] Three years later, Judge Fisher continued to champion the need for social centers in the Lawndale community, observing, "In my court, I have often noticed that Jewish fathers and mothers have no control over their children, who go on corrupt paths."[136] He believed the social centers had the potential to reconnect parents with their children—to close the

The move from Maxwell Street. Construction of the Jewish People's Institute in Lawndale, Chicago, December 3, 1926. *Chicago History Museum, ICHi-18850, Chicago Architectural Photographing Co.*

ever-widening generational gap. In 1926, the JPI moved with the Jewish population to Lawndale after twenty-two years of service in the Maxwell Street district, signifying a symbolic closing of the West Side ghetto.

From 1900 to 1925, a portion of the Jewish youth deviated from the values and religion that their Orthodox parents and grandparents held dear. Whether the boys' gangs formed to obtain greater economic mobility, to ensure self-protection against their anti-Semitic neighbors or simply to gain a sense of belonging, they forced the Chicago Jewish community to grasp a reality they did not wish to face. Questions of police protection and prejudice arose. Shame and disappointment pulsed through the pages of the Yiddish press while the proliferation of Jewish delinquency also attracted the attention of the *Chicago Tribune*. From within the community, Jews began to voice their opinions of how to right the wrongs of the "Americanized" and unprincipled Jewry. Holding the parents of these children more accountable, reforming and strengthening the Jewish education system and expanding the community's institutional infrastructure were all approaches that members advocated. Despite all the awareness raised and reforms proposed, the elevation of the Jewish community's social and economic standing in Chicago, evident in the migration of the Jews from the West Side, proved to be the definitive element that diminished juvenile delinquency and street gangs. Nevertheless, it did not and could not erase the hundreds of existing juvenile delinquents, some of whom looked to older Jews, like Davey Miller, to make the transition into the world of organized crime.

3

"HOW TO MAKE A GANGSTER"

From Juvenile Delinquent to Organized Criminal in the Chicago Underworld

It makes a Chicago businessman weary now to chew the rag with him about the "c'rupshun" in the city. He's heard an' read about it till he don't want to see the word any more. [137]
—*A man of the Chicago underworld in conversation with journalist Josiah Flynt, 1900*

At the start of the 1930s, *Collier's National Weekly* garnered a readership of nearly two million Americans. [138] Known for its vibrant, colorful illustrations and for a cast of writers that famously included Winston Churchill, the magazine began a newfound resurgence in the 1930s under editor William L. Chenery. Beginning in 1924, Chenery placed fiction at the cornerstone of *Collier's* and strayed away from its traditional orientation of muckraking, crusader journalism that dated back to the magazine's 1888 founding. [139] In 1933, *Collier's* sold for five cents a piece and featured short stories by authors such as George Agnew Chamberlain, reflecting Chenery's successful emphasis on works of fiction. However, the September 2 edition of that year had a strikingly different cover with a distinct purpose: to grab the attention of its readers. A blond-haired, blue-eyed toddler, clad in a diaper and a white T-shirt, lay atop a pool table. With eyebrows furled and eyes intently fixed on the next potential shot, the infant clenched the cue stick in his hands. This juxtaposition no doubt made parents cringe. The baby was too fierce to be their child and too young to be playing in a poolroom, and yet, it may have felt surprisingly close to home, particularly in a vice-ridden metropolis like Chicago that was well into its thirteenth year of Prohibition.

In "How to Make a Gangster," the article that accompanied the sensational illustration, writer William G. Shepherd explored the Chicago underworld—the shadow of the city—and the relationship between boys' gangs and older criminals. The nationally known staff writer for *Collier's* interviewed and combined the perspectives of Chicago Jewish gangster Davey Miller and sociologist John Landesco to share with the readers how children became hardened criminals.[140] *Collier's* high position in American society during the 1930s, as well as the report's front-page placement, demonstrates the seriousness of and fascination with gangsters and vice in the early twentieth century. The inclusion of Shepherd and Davey Miller's conversation catapulted Chicago Jewish criminals onto a national level and hints at their involvement in vice. However, exploring Jewish criminal involvement in the various professional crime ventures and positioning the gangsters and the Jewish community in relation to the entire portrait of Chicago vice is not yet possible. First, an overview of the Chicago underworld, including the district known to some as "Bloody Maxwell," as well as an analysis of the transition from juvenile delinquency to organized crime, is imperative.

I

"The city is a recognized haunt of tramps and thieves," proclaimed sociologist Josiah Flynt in 1901, "and where tramps and thieves congregate by permission in large numbers, the municipal authorities are not 'on the level.'"[141] By 1900, Chicago's underworld truly had developed into an entangled web of organized crime, where gangsters, government officials and policemen intersected one another in a system of payoffs and favors. Poolrooms, saloons, dance halls, resorts and houses of ill repute proliferated. Gambling, prostitution and immoralities of all sorts flourished. Indeed, its alarming degree of organization set it apart from the comparatively inefficient, adolescent street gangs. Yet the mass development of the city's underworld had its roots in the prior century, dating back as early as the 1830s—the time of the municipality's incorporation. In Chicago's infancy, betting on horse races was the most salient form of gambling, and on its coattails came the prostitutes and pimps.[142] Their arrival was met with some concern, and in 1835, the town's board of trustees imposed a fine of twenty-five dollars on any person found guilty of keeping a bawdy house.[143] However, the haunts of the town's shadow continued to mature in spite of these measures. Liquor trafficking skyrocketed, and gunmen, pickpockets, thieves and ruffians filled out the lower echelons of the city. As the need for vice grew, so too did the number of tippling houses, saloons and gambling dens.[144]

At the 1857 Cook County Maine Law Convention, Reverend Archibald Kenyon of the Tabernacle Church of West Chicago presented a report on the city's iniquities—especially liquor trafficking—and their effects on morality. The January 30 edition of the *Chicago Tribune* published the report in its entirety. Kenyon believed that it was time to "arouse the public to the fearful extent of intemperance," which was surely the catalyst for corruption.[145] The report cited approximately 600 liquor establishments in Chicago, 388 of which operated without licenses in 1856. Additionally, Kenyon and the rest of the committee connected the liquor trafficking business and its saloons to gambling—"where time is wasted" and "morals destroyed"—and to houses of prostitution.[146] The proposed resolution called for an ordinance mirroring the Maine Law of 1851, which largely restricted the sale of all alcoholic beverages in the New England state. Yet it was a call for temperance that would not be answered in nineteenth-century Chicago. Instead, the Chicago underworld continued to grow as the 1800s progressed. The expansion of the city's infrastructure near the turn of the century challenged the underworld to keep pace.[147] It did just that and more, enveloping the Twenty-second Precinct on the West Side—the Maxwell Street district—and the Jewish community.

On February 6, 1906, the *Chicago Tribune* declared the Maxwell Street district to be the "wickedest district in the world, where scores of men and women are murdered every year."[148] This dramatic proclamation was also the title of the day's front-page story. The cosmopolitan, less-than-two-mile-long district known to many as "Bloody Maxwell" of course included the Jewish ghetto. The reporter painted with words this notorious segment of the underworld: "With the approach of night…the lights in the saloons begin to be lit, and the tough ones make ready for the biggest hours of the twenty-four," though he cautioned that it was unsafe during the daytime, too.[149] It was here that the "worst kind" of robbers, thieves and murderers matured and thrived in the face of an inadequate police force. Journalist and author Herbert Asbury agreed with the paper's assessment of the district. He maintained that along with the Thirty-eighth Precinct on the North

Side, the Twenty-second Precinct was the most notorious area of the city at the turn of the twentieth century. Compared to Bloody Maxwell, however, the Thirty-eighth Precinct seemed a "paradise."[150]

The underworld's crawl into the Jewish ghetto in concert with the transformation of the West Side levee did not go unnoticed. As with other community issues, the *Daily Jewish Courier* was at the forefront of educating its readers about these startling changes. The official organ of the Orthodox Jewry warned its brethren of a threatening, new and very real plague—white slavery—that terrorized their daughters. The newspaper devoted a double-column editorial to the matter in the fall of 1907. The *Courier's* publisher, M.P. Ginzburg, asserted, "The proximity of the West Side levee is a source of danger to hundreds of Jewish daughters and is a disgrace to the respectable Jewish people living nearby."[151] Men were luring the girls away from their families in a variety of ways, including marriages under aliases, to sell them into prostitution. In several of the Maxwell Street district's brothels, both the keepers and their young strumpets were Jewish. The article emphasized the shame that these gangsters brought to the Jewish name. They "blacken[ed] the name of hundreds of thousands of peaceful and thrifty Jewish citizens in Chicago…by their disgraceful conduct."[152] By shaming the Jewish men involved in white slave trafficking, the community sought to disassociate themselves from the vice. More than anything, they wanted to reassure the Chicago gentiles that it was not a fault of the entire community but rather a problem concerning a subgroup that the Jews recognized and would eradicate. The underworld's move into the Maxwell Street district and the evil growing within their own community was an affront to the Jews' pride, as was their children's involvement in street gangs.

Yet like the problem of juvenile delinquency, efforts of the "upperworld"— respectable society—to reform white slavery and other criminal pursuits were often futile. Legislation, such as the Vagrancy Law of 1906, failed to quell the undesirables of Chicago.[153] So, too, were earlier actions taken by Mayor Carter Harrison Jr., who served from 1897 to 1905 and again from 1911 to 1915. In 1900, for example, the mayor ordered the midnight closing of all the city's saloons, which included the halting of liquor sales, music and the operation of the venues' slot machines.[154] Three years later, Chicago's chief of police Francis O'Neill persuaded Mayor Harrison to revoke the licenses of three corrupt saloons, including that of A.H. and B. Goldberg on 59 South Halsted Street.[155] While the proprietors' nationality and religion were unverifiable, the surname hints at their being members of the Jewish community, particularly given the establishment's West Side locale. Despite the saloons' overwhelming compliance with the decrees, the measures did little to impede the underworld. In an interview with the *Chicago Tribune* around the time of the 1900 saloon order, Mayor Harrison rightly admitted, "Vice will always exist in the city of Chicago. It cannot be entirely stamped out—not as long as human nature is as it is."[156]

One explanation for the Chicago underworld's resistance to reform lies in the blurred divide between the upperworld and the shadows. In 1903, a commission assembled to investigate allegations of graft in the Chicago Police Department absolved the force of wrongdoing and praised them for their valiant efforts against criminal activity.[157] Yet just a year later, an investigation by Captain Alexander Piper and his team of New York detectives found an extremely inefficient and undisciplined Chicago Police Department. Findings included numerous patrolmen deserting their posts and even drinking in the saloons they were to monitor.[158] To compound this unprofessionalism was the lingering and growing belief in the reality of police protection and criminal payoffs. These agreements between the gangsters and detectives facilitated the criminals' ability to escape the law if they periodically gave adequate money to the policemen. Furthermore, these arrangements allowed the underworld to flourish in the face of reform efforts.

At the Maxwell Street police station in the early twentieth century, Jewish second-class detective Sergeant Michael Weisbaum was at the center of crime control in Bloody Maxwell but is also exemplary of this sort of clandestine relationship that frequently prevailed. In an investigative report of the Chicago Crime Commission on August 15, 1914, an inspector wrote about the connection between Weisbaum and local pickpockets. "I spoke to…officer Weisbaum at the Maxwell Street Station, in reference to pickpockets in the district. [He] Informed me that there was not one pickpocket in the district. On making inquiries, I was told that Weisbaum knew at least one hundred pickpockets, in the vicinity of Halsted and Maxwell and that he protected them as far as he was able"—meaning within his station's jurisdiction.[159] Though it is difficult to say how trustworthy the investigator's informant ("son of Coleburn") was, the claim is far easier to believe than Weisbaum's of a pickpocket-free district, especially after knowing the prevalence of Jewish pickpockets around the ghetto at this time.

A separate report from Investigator Friedner in November 1914 further reinforces Weisbaum's collusion with the city's criminals. At Frisch's Café, a popular hangout for the local undesirables, Investigator Friedner had a drink with the owner's son-in-law. He told Friedner, "Weissbaum [*sic*] was after getting two of the boys from Lehrman's joint out of trouble, and it cost them [the railroad thieves] $200.00 to square themselves."[160] The testimony provides a concrete example of graft in action throughout the Maxwell Street district. Additionally, it demonstrates how the boundary between the upper- and underworlds was truly obscured because even those designated to protect society, such as policemen, chose to protect the gangsters, too. Just five days later, for example, another investigator noted, "The way that all the crooks talk to Mike Weissbaum [sic], it looks very much like he was [sic] their leader."[161] However, police protection was only one explanation for the development of the underworld on the West Side in spite of various reform efforts.

There was also an inexhaustible stock of juvenile delinquents, including the Jewish adolescents showcased in chapter two who were intent on transitioning to organized crime—hoping to make their name known throughout the Chicago underworld. Thus, analyzing this transition— including the delinquents' various motivations—will advance a more thorough justification for why the city's vices persisted and set the stage for exploring Jewish involvement in the more organized crime ventures.

II

At the Maxwell Street Police Station, where detectives arrested nearly sixty boys under the age of ten per month in 1906, policemen understood that to fight the underworld with any success, they had to target the boys' gangs.[162] After all, if a young Jewish gangster were caught early enough and tried in the juvenile court system, he might crawl out from the city's haunts in time. If he continued to drift through the years with no arrest, however, he was likely to be a "full-fledged criminal" by the age of nineteen.[163] The 1913 *Chicago Tribune* article that stated this claim landed on the paper's front page. The report called for parents to be more aware of their children and of the grave danger that these boys' gangs posed to the city. They were the "greatest schools for crime," and a figurative graduation from such groups signified a long criminal career.[164] Of course, there were innumerable individual reasons for a juvenile of Maxwell Street to make the transition to organized criminal, but there were several recurring factors that increased his likelihood. Those elements worth exploring include the child's economic mobility, environment and "hero worship" of the older gangsters.

The more economically successful a juvenile delinquent was in a street gang, the more enticing the notion of continuing his career in vice. Given the dilapidated conditions of the ghetto's tenements, which often brought the Jewish children to the streets in the first place, the child perhaps witnessed firsthand his parents' toil and struggle to climb Chicago's social and economic ladder in a respectable manner. According to sociologist John Landesco, "The older gangster…lures with promises of bigger money, protection and manly vices…who have at their fingers' ends the sources of spending money for pleasures to be achieved either within the neighborhood or in the wide metropolis."[165] Thus, despite the risks attached to involving oneself deeper in the underworld, it did present the young gangsters with a chance for greater prosperity and more experiences that would otherwise be unavailable. Furthermore, since the older gangsters were often from the same neighborhood as the delinquents they targeted, they understood what the children did not have and emphasized that what they desired the most was attainable through vice.

The environment of the juvenile delinquent—both physical and emotional—also had a great influence on his decision of whether to pursue a full-time career in crime. Many studies have demonstrated that gang activity bloomed more in the city's slum areas, which certainly included the Jewish ghetto. Lack of "breathing spots" and playgrounds as well as insufficient recreational and vocational facilities combined to create a physical environment for the child conducive to straying away from a path of morality.[166] While contemplating solutions to ease Chicago's crime problem, the city council's Committee on Crime, reporting in 1915, recommended that the "Board of Education enlarge its facilities (a) for vocational education; and (b) for vocational guidance…and that juvenile probationers be required to attend such school during the period of probation."[167] For the children of the ghetto and other slum areas, inadequate education and guidance equated more time spent on the streets and greater interaction with gangsters recruiting the next class of criminals.

There was a profound lack of guidance in these children's lives at home, too. The parents worked long hours, leaving the children alone longer than was healthy for those so young. As a result, these parents paid little attention to their children's lives and were surprisingly unaware of the changes occurring, such as a growing disinterest in school and more time spent with boys' gangs in undesirable locations like the neighborhood restaurants, saloons and poolrooms.[168] Nevertheless, even the utmost parental attention could induce a child to deviate from morality, particularly in the homes of the Russian Orthodox Jewry—the majority of the ghetto's inhabitants in the early twentieth century. As I alluded to in chapter one, youth from these families often rebelled from the ways of their immigrant parents. The elders held on to the Old World beliefs and culture that they had left behind. Meanwhile, their children had no connection to the religious orthodoxy and little desire to re-create a lifestyle steeped in the traditions of the Russian shtetl. Consequently, neither family member could understand the other, and a growing, intergenerational gap emerged. This type of distancing also contributed to a lack of guidance and thus a greater opportunity for the children to wander the city's streets.

In the Maxwell Street district, there was no want of saloons or poolrooms. Though the Jewish juvenile delinquents could not enter all of the establishments, Jane Addams once noted to an audience of parents with elementary school–aged children that the leaders of boys' gangs knew "what poolrooms never are raided in search of boys under 18, and what saloons sell liquor to minors."[169] This speaks again to the close connection between boys' gangs and organized crime in Chicago. It would be impossible to ascertain which saloons and poolrooms protected against raids on minors, but there were several with Jewish proprietors in the area. Considering the tightknit mentality of the Jewish community in the Maxwell Street district, it is likely some of these places opened their doors to their younger Jewish counterparts. There was Frisch's restaurant at 1105 South Halsted Street, which, according to an August 8, 1914 investigator's report, was a hangout for pickpockets—"all Jews."[170] Then there was Bartelstein's poolroom and restaurant at Twelfth and Newberry Streets—another popular hangout for the Jewish pickpockets. Others included Artkin's saloon, near the Maxwell Street police station, and Abraham's saloon, owned by the brother of former ghetto alderman Emanuel Abrahams, at 921 West Twelfth Street.[171] Of course, this is not an exhaustive list of the establishments in Bloody Maxwell run by Jews in the early twentieth century—merely a sampling.

The *Daily Jewish Forward*, a Yiddish labor newspaper on the West Side, took notice of the negative influence these places were having on their community's children in 1924, with particular emphasis on poolrooms. The newspaper warned that once a youngster began to frequent a poolroom and consort with its regulars, the child was likely to adopt the habitués—"habits, mode of speech, codes, combined with their swagger ways of easy existence."[172] Consequently, the author saw the poolroom as a platform for the transformation of a child into a professional criminal. He pleaded for such a boy's parents to keep a closer eye on their child and for the sister to save her brother by notifying mother and father of his poolroom associations.

However, the lack of familial guidance made children increasingly vulnerable to other influences, and as they frequented the saloons, poolrooms and restaurants, the older Jewish gangsters filled the void of "role model." As with most children who look up to their parents, actors or superheroes, the juvenile delinquents were also subject to hero worship. In fact, this was a strong motivation for choosing a life in the underworld. They admired the senior gangsters of the poolroom and became fascinated with their power. They saw men with money, women and beautiful automobiles. Accordingly, some boys began "to emulate them…to live as easy as they [the gangsters] do without the necessity of going to work in a store or factory every day of the week."[173] The notion of hero worship as an explanation for the transition from juvenile delinquency to organized crime was also central to the September 2, 1933 edition of *Collier's Weekly* and its cover story, "How to Make a Gangster." However, for author William Shepherd, the hero was not just the seasoned gangster but also peers of the juvenile delinquent. He agreed with John Landesco, who told him, "Their heroes are the boys of the neighborhood who turn out to be gangster killers. They become legends which inspire."[174]

One such hero of the underworld who grew up in the ghetto was Davey Miller—boxing referee, restaurant owner, gambler and political fixer extraordinaire—whose brother, Hirschie, was a major bootlegger in Chicago.[175] Despite Davey's proclamation in his interview with Shepherd that he was "not a gangster," several incidents suggest that he was. In 1924, Dion O'Banion—founder and then leader of the North Side Gang—shot at both brothers. O'Banion "feared none, but watched for many," including the Miller brothers.[176] The following year, federal agents arrested Davey, his brother, Policeman Harry Miller and others in an "alleged plot to extort bribe money from a peddler of dope."[177] The investigators charged Davey with conspiracy. Moreover, sociologist John Landesco listed Davey Miller under "vice," "gambling" and "booze" for criminals with "no record in [the] Identification Bureau but [with] other record of conviction."[178] In short, it was safe to say that Davey Miller was a gangster. While this attempt to clear his name may have been the sole reason for agreeing to an interview with a nationally circulated magazine, his comments do provide us with a unique opportunity to hear the verified words of a Chicago Jewish gangster.

Portions of his interview were stories that incited awe in readers. For instance, he told of Al Capone stopping by his restaurant in the weeks following O'Banion's gunshot. According to Miller, Capone told him, "Dave,

Dion shouldn't have done that to you and I've told him so. I told him I thought he owed you about $5,000 for doctor bills...so he turned five grand over to me and here it is."[179] Though only substantiated through Davey's words, it was nonetheless an interaction and an example of a relationship that movies are made of. Other parts of his conversation with Shepherd afford an enriched understanding of just how a gangster is made in the ghetto. When asked how gangsters grow, Davey replied, "They can't help growing, the way things are here in this town."[180] This might suggest that, to Miller, taking part in the underworld was a necessary evil and reality of a boy growing up in the ghetto. Yet whether making this transition was a boy's chance to improve his physical and emotional environment, gain greater economic mobility or simply emulate the older gangsters, there always seemed to be a new stock of criminals, Jewish and gentile, eager to fill the Chicago underworld. Perhaps Chicago Jewish gangster Davey Miller provided the greatest insight of all: "It isn't in a kid who's born and lives in one of these gang districts not to be some sort of a gangster, if he's lively and lucky enough. It's about the only thing a kid can get a chance to be."[181]

4

"PROTECT THE GIRL!"

White Slavery, Prostitution and the Chicago Jewry, 1900–1920

It is a terrible thing that Jews in Chicago are among the leaders in the trade in human virtue. We must rescue the weak of our community and forestall their falling further.[182]
—*Dr. Emil G. Hirsch, speaking at the inaugural service of the People's Synagogue association, November 1912*

On February 1, 1912, Phil Friedman married Rose, a Jewish girl who lived with her parents at 1244 South Carpenter Street, just north of Taylor Street on the near West Side. Phil was twenty-two years old. Rose was merely seventeen. Yet notwithstanding their difference in age, the union seemed normal. However, within weeks of their marriage, Friedman's true intentions became apparent. He "had her [Rose] hustle out of Mattie Maybaum's house of ill-fame [at] 2004 Dearborn Street"—a block in Chicago notorious for its numerous brothels in the early twentieth century.[183] Less than a month later, on March 12, Sergeant Max Weisbaum of the Maxwell Street Police Station rescued Rose from the resort, and Phil fled the city, bound for Buffalo, New York. With a state warrant authorized, Officer Weisbaum arrested Friedman and brought him back to Chicago in May of the same year. He charged the miscreant with pandering—the pimping or procuring of prostitutes. The defendant entered a plea of guilty, and on May 22, Judge Dicker of the Maxwell Street court sentenced him to one year in the house of correction and issued a $1,000 fine.[184]

Of course, the case's fortunate resolution did not come from the work of Officer Weisbaum alone. Rather, it was the direct product of the Chicago Committee of Fifteen's investigations and part of a larger and highly sensationalized reform effort in the city, spearheaded by then assistant state's attorney Clifford Roe, to combat the problem of prostitution.[185] Originally founded in 1908, the Committee of Fifteen attempted to suppress pandering in the city. The private organization sent investigators to the various vice districts to collect personal observations, including the names, phone numbers and addresses of those engaged in the illicit business of prostitution. Upon gathering enough evidence, the committee would contact the appropriate policemen, who, like Officer Weisbaum, would then bring the criminals to court.[186] The Committee of Fifteen worked in tandem with the Chicago Vice Commission, which boldly recommended in its 1911 report: "Constant and persistent repression of prostitution the immediate method: Absolute annihilation the ultimate ideal."[187] However, after the city's government initially refused to establish a morals commission, one of two primary proposals presented in the 1911 report, the Committee of Fifteen took a more prominent role in the anti-prostitution crusade, thus bringing criminals like Phil Friedman to justice.[188]

As with the trial's investigatory history, the particulars of *People v. Friedman* were not unique among other cases of white slavery—meaning coerced prostitution.[189] Rose's and Friedman's profiles, particularly their Jewish heritage, as well as the latter's method of procurement, were commonplace in the tarnished world of white slave trafficking. In turn, the story serves as an archetype for this variety of vice in Chicago and illuminates the active role that Jewish gangsters played. In fact, the city's key reformers during this period consistently emphasized and singled out the involvement of Eastern European Jews in this traffic and as owners of the disorderly houses, which allowed prostitution to flourish in Chicago. Though reformers unduly blamed these Jews for the prolific white slave trade, their involvement nonetheless is significant because it challenged leaders of the Jewish community to take initiative in the reform effort and to confront the morality of their people in an attempt to guard against themselves and prevailing anti-Semitic sentiment.

I

In his September 1909 interview with the *Chicago Tribune*, reform leader and former assistant state's attorney Clifford G. Roe rightly proclaimed that white slavery was "as old as Babylon."[190] To the Chicago public, however, it remained a dark and hidden feature of a familiar and commercialized vice years into the twentieth century. It was in the 1860s and 1870s that prostitution developed into the greatest and most lucrative business of the Chicago underworld. Based on newspaper accounts and court papers, journalist Herbert Asbury estimated that there were between 200 and 250 brothels in Chicago during the 1860s. Yet despite this shocking approximation, contemporary Chicagoans generally considered prostitution to be an ineluctable part of society and accepted its existence so long as the vice remained in the city's background.[191] All the same, not everyone stood idly by. There were certainly organizations in the late nineteenth century that began to crusade against the evils of white slavery, not only in Chicago, but also in cities across the country.

Following English journalist William T. Stead's 1885 article entitled "The Maiden Tribute of Modern Babylon," the Woman's Christian Temperance Union (WCTU) became one such organization. In his report, Stead exposed a system in England in which men drugged, imprisoned and raped impoverished girls.[192] In 1893, after visiting Chicago, Stead wrote *If Christ Came to Chicago*. In this 472-page account of the city's vice, he related the existence of the same English system in Chicago. "The procuress plies her trade in Chicago as in other large cities, preying upon youth and inexperience," Stead observed.[193] Appalled by these revelations, Frances Willard, a leader of the WCTU, created a new subdivision in the organization, first called the Department of Social Purity, to fight against sexual violence and forced prostitution in America.[194] However on the whole, the speeches and campaigns of Willard, the WTCU and other nineteenth-century reformers did not appear to awaken Chicago or its Jewish community to the horrors and seriousness of the white slave trade that accompanied the commercialized vice of the underworld.

Indeed, white slavery remained, more or less, in the city's background until April 1907. That month, the acclaimed *McClure's* magazine published an article by journalist George Kibbe Turner that startled Chicago "out of her usual attitude of indifference toward commercialized vice."[195] In "The City of Chicago: A Study of the Great Immoralities," Turner brought the darkest elements of the underworld to light—not because crime was unique to this city but rather because it was representative of the decadence most urban areas faced.[196] He introduced Chicago prostitution as a $20 million business that employed at least ten thousand professional harlots. Oftentimes these women never saw the revenue because proprietors of hotels, brothels, dancehalls and saloons exploited their earnings. Yet Turner mentioned another party that took the women's wages: "men—largely Russian Jews—who deal in women for the trade."[197] He maintained that these men—loosely organized across the major metropolises of the country—target women of the same nationality to sell into the houses of ill fame in the city's West Side Levee.[198] To be sure, investigators were never able to verify a national organization of Jewish white slavers so the operative term was "loosely." However, the tactics employed were so invariable from city to city that it gave the trade this appearance.[199] Nevertheless, most striking was the indictment of Russian Jews who sold their religious sisters to the houses for, on average, fifty dollars each, which the women would then have to "work" to pay back.[200] These deplorable findings at once speak to the trust members of the Jewish community placed with one another, particularly those from Eastern Europe living in the ghetto. It is important to remember that by the time of the article's publication, most of the German Jews from the first great wave of immigration had ascended the social and economic ladder of the city, while the second, primarily Russian and Polish, wave of immigrants remained in the West Side slums. This helps to explain how a man like Phil Friedman, in the opening example, was able to convince Rose to marry with the consent of her parents. Friedman promised a better situation and future for their daughter than they could provide—a ticket out of the ghetto.

The impact of George Kibbe Turner's muckraking article on the city of Chicago, and especially on its Jewish community, should not be understated. It sparked a large-scale movement against the white slave trade that would endure for more than a decade and challenged Chicago Jewry to confront their complicity. In the summer of 1907, Illinois state's attorney John Wayman entrusted assistant counsel Clifford Roe with the task of prosecuting those involved in the trade. Roe had great success, and the courts convicted, fined and imprisoned many procurers. Curiously, within months, politicians significantly diminished Roe's work, perhaps because of the inextricable ties between the city's government and the underworld.[201] Nevertheless, he remained determined to root out the white slave trade. Others pledged their support and funded his investigations, including members and organizational bodies of the Jewish community.[202]

The *Daily Jewish Courier*, as with the proliferation of juvenile delinquency, led the way in educating the community about the increasing rise of white slavery in its neighborhood. As it was the organ of Orthodox Jewry, this does not come as a surprise. In contrast to the German Reform Jews, the targets of the crusade—Eastern European Jews—were by and large religiously conservative, so the newspaper spoke directly to the families of the criminals. On November 5, 1907, the *Courier* proclaimed, "The members of our community were not fully aware of this growing menace but now that our columns have taken up the crusade, the citizenry is fully aroused, and a demand for action forthcoming."[203] However, the action would not come solely from the Orthodox Jewry. The Chicago chapter of B'nai B'rith, a worldwide Jewish service organization, satisfied the demand by establishing a committee to expose those involved in the white slave trade on the West Side.[204] Its president, Adolf Kraus, emigrated from Bohemia in 1865 and became the international president of B'nai B'rith in 1905.[205] His prominent position in the organization, as well as his Central European roots, is noteworthy. He demonstrated that this movement would involve the entire Jewish community, not just the Russian Jews. They chose Clifford Roe to head their campaign, which meant that the organization helped to fund his investigations. This partnership continued into the following year.

The drive to clean up the West Side district heightened as the one-year anniversary of George Kibbe Turner's article approached. Chief of Police George Shippy brought in a new force of men to the police station situated in the West Side levee, endeavoring to begin a graft-less era of enforcement. Police inspector Edward McCann, previously from the Twenty-second Street station, raided hundreds of bawdy houses and saloons with concert halls that employed women. While gangsters resisted and even petitioned for his transfer, McCann declared, "I do not mean to let up on them [criminals] at any time. The vicious element and undesirable levee character must step aside, for decency demands it."[206] Yet less than a year later, many would come to question his own decency, and he became the defendant in a trial that illuminated like never before the Jewish ties to the prostitution business.

Meanwhile, 1908 also opened the eyes of Chicago wider to the ins and outs of white slavery, as Roe's prosecutions and newspaper coverage combined to further sensationalize the matter. A July 26 *Chicago Tribune* article did just that. The report opened by boldly declaring "Chicago…the greatest market for white slavery on the continent."[207] It featured quotations from Roe and U.S. district attorney Edwin Sims, the latter of whom serves to demonstrate the seriousness of the trafficking and the national attention it garnered.

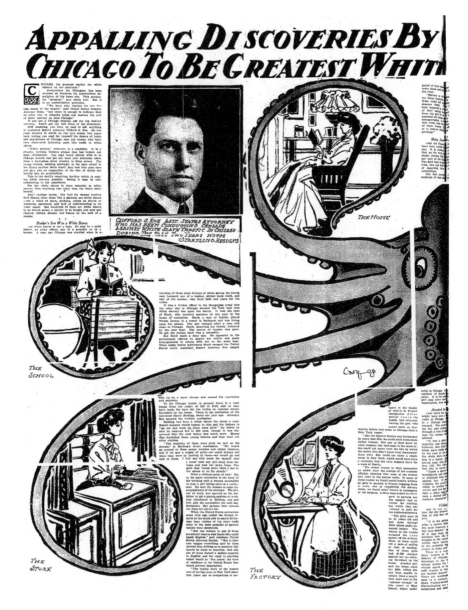

The metaphoric tentacles of white slavery, wrapped around vulnerable girls throughout Chicago, 1908. *From the* Chicago Tribune, *July 26, 1908.*

Additionally, the reporter's language epitomized what became a mainstay of white slave reform rhetoric—comparisons to chattel slavery: "Hundreds of them are white slaves in its literal sense; a chattel to be bought and sold and chained, robbed, abused and beaten by the lash of a master."[208] Sociologist Brian Donovan observed that urban reformers utilized this comparison to intimate that a movement as spirited as the one against chattel slavery was necessary.[209] This tactic effectively grabbed the emotional attention of many readers, as did the melodramatic nature of the article's layout.

Visually, the column depicted an octopus with its long and winding tentacles wrapped around illustrations that portrayed the places where girls were most vulnerable. The octopus, representing the white slave trade, preyed primarily on poor immigrant girls at department stores, factories, theatrical agencies, railroad depots and farms. In addition to false promises of marriage, sociologist Walter Reckless explained, "the white slaves were said to be lured by promises of luxury…by flattering attention, appeals to vanity, the dazzle and whirl of bright lights in cities [used to lure farm girls] and sometimes by forced abduction."[210] In department stores, for example, opulent clothing and wealthy customers surrounded fatigued female workers who received meager salaries and could not afford the stores' luxuries. Most dwelled on greater futures and lovers who would save them from their loneliness. Due to the accessibility of these stores, procurers exploited these vulnerabilities and provided the girls with a newfound sense of confidence and affection, assuring them that they would enjoy the splendors of life they deserved.[211] Equally troubling was the role that some theatrical agencies played in this trade. Conspiring with disorderly houses, the agencies advertised for pretty girls and promised large salaries.[212] As journalist Karen Abbott wrote, "Advertisements in newspapers seeking secretaries and clerks and leads for musical productions were best read skeptically."[213] It would appear then that no family was safe from the reaches of white slavery, particularly Eastern European Jews who were among the most destitute. Naturally, reformers emphasized this vulnerability to heighten the public's awareness.

Legislative reform passed in July 1908. Illinois became the first state to make pandering a crime. The bill fined first offenders $1,000 or sentenced them to a minimum of six months in the house of correction. Among those who went to Springfield on behalf of the innovative law was Adolf Kraus of B'nai B'rith, who continued to play an integral role in the reform effort.[214] Another Jew, Dr. David Blaustein, also entered the fight against prostitution in 1908. Born in Lida, Russia, on May 5, 1866, Blaustein first immigrated to New York, where he gained prominence in various Jewish civic organizations.[215] In November 1908, after serving as president of the National Jewish Social Workers' Association and as a member of the Educational Alliance, he took the position as superintendent of the Chicago

Hebrew Institute, a vital West Side community center that promoted the Americanization of Eastern European immigrants.[216] However, Blaustein was ambitious and shouldered another role. Upon his arrival in Chicago, he helped to found the Committee of Three—the predecessor to the Committee of Fifteen—that worked to suppress the white slave traffic.[217] In contrast to Adolf Kraus, the condemnation of the Eastern European Jews was more personally relevant to Blaustein given his birthplace and perhaps explains why he became involved in the movement so quickly. As 1909 fast approached, Clifford Roe resigned from the state's attorney's office and pursued his string of pandering prosecutions in private practice. Additionally, Kraus and Blaustein continued to represent the Jewish community in the struggle to rid their people of procurers and whorehouse proprietors and to mend the Jews' damaged standing in the city. Yet nothing could prepare the Chicago Jewry for the testimony of brothers Julius and Louis Frank, who redefined the image of a gangster just a few months later.

II

On January 30, 1909, the *Chicago Tribune* summarized some of the actions police inspector Edward McCann had taken since relocating to the West Side Levee district. Among these were the "abolition of dozens of immoral houses, with full control of those remaining" and the "enforcement of the pandering law."[218] Reformers and civic organizations alike praised McCann for the strides made in cleaning up the levee. Concurrently, however, state's attorney John Wayman began his own investigations into various police districts to expose the officials who were in collusion with the underworld. Midway through the year, Wayman assessed the Desplaines Street station—McCann's precinct. Through this investigation, the state's attorney amassed considerable evidence against Edward McCann—an eighteen-year officer—to take legal action, much to the dismay of the public and the denial of the policeman. On July 24, the Cook County grand jury indicted Edward McCann on ten charges of "bribe taking and malfeasance in office," which "left Chicago in a state of chaotic expectancy."[219] Supporters of the inspector contended that it was a plot to bring down McCann because he was now a threat to the underworld. Others believed lower-ranking officials feared McCann would soon replace George Shippy as chief of police and cited that as motivation.[220]

Portrait of police inspector Edward McCann sitting at a desk in Chicago, 1909. *Chicago History Museum, DN-0054826, Chicago Daily News, Inc.*

Despite these theories, testimony mounted against the police inspector. Louis and Julius Frank, Jewish brothers from the West Side, emerged as the chief witnesses in the trial. They were popular saloonkeepers at Halsted and West Madison Streets, where undesirables of the West Side flocked. More importantly, they also owned real estate "said by McCann to be used for immoral purposes"—i.e., prostitution.[221] In their confessions, the brothers detailed an alleged system of graft in which keepers of disorderly houses regularly paid protection money to Inspector McCann. Julius Frank affirmed, "It is

An artist's rendering of Louis Frank, displayed in an article regarding the levee investigation, 1909. *From the Chicago Tribune, July 27, 1909.*

Charged with conspiracy to violate Prohibition laws, Mike "de Pike" Heitler (left) sits near deputy United States marshal John Oros (right) in Chicago, 1923. *Chicago History Museum, DN-0076268, Chicago Daily News, Inc.*

true I am the man who collected the graft and turned it over to Inspector McCann. I can say from my own knowledge that there is not one resort on the west side that did not pay protection money to McCann."[222]

Louis Frank also collected protection money for the officer. After moving to the West Side police district, McCann told Louis that for twenty dollars, "they [payers] would get protection from arrest, unexpected raids and hounding by patrolmen and detectives." Louis continued, "The inspector had a book in which he kept track of every inmate of the houses in the district and every keeper. It was in going over this that he found that some buildings sheltered more than one place" and consequently charged those owners forty dollars.[223] Moreover, Louis asserted that Mike "de Pike" Heitler, Jewish vice lord and a notorious keeper, was one of McCann's right-hand men and cited several other individuals, too.[224]

Though ancillary to the Frank's testimony, it demonstrates the number of people complicit in this system, the extent of vice on the West Side and the complexities of the trial. On September 21, closing arguments commenced. Policemen and community members verified the Frank brothers' "good character," as the truthfulness of their testimony had come under attack by McCann's counsel.[225] The jury delivered a verdict of guilty after just one night's adjournment. McCann's counsel successfully appealed to the Supreme Court for a new trial, but judges ultimately upheld the conviction. Wayman's victory landed police inspector Edward McCann in the state penitentiary.[226]

Coverage of the case regularly crowded the front pages of the *Chicago Tribune*. Louis and Julius Frank's central role in the system of paid protection only confirmed what had been known for two years: Jews were omnipresent in the white slave trade. Yet it was not simply the Frank brothers' high-profile involvement or the heightened exposure of West Side vice that incited uproar throughout the Chicago Jewish community. It was the fact that Julius Frank was the president of the Orthodox Congregation Anshe Kalvaria while he and Louis ran the brothels. This presented a major dichotomy between the morality of Judaism and the unprincipled activities of the underworld. Located at Twelfth and South Union Streets in the heart of the ghetto, Anshe Kalvaria was reportedly one of the leading Jewish synagogues in the city.[227] Furthermore, its location and Orthodox tradition suggests that the Frank brothers were from Eastern Europe—in line with George Kibbe Turner's findings—because most Germans were Reform Jews and out of the Maxwell Street area by this time.

Dr. Emil Hirsch, rabbi of the Sinai Congregation and advocate of Reform Judaism, utilized the *Forward* to condemn both the Franks and Anshe Kalvaria and echoed the overall sentiment of the Jewish community.[228] Out of the trial came the alarming statistic that Jews controlled 75 percent of the white slave trade in Chicago. Hirsch reflected:

> *The shame would not be so overwhelming if the thing stopped there. For after all we could say: "what can we do if such creatures persist in calling themselves Jews?" But we could say this only if these outcasts had remained where they belong and had no standing in the Jewish community of this city. When these men, however, fill public offices in the Jewish community…and are designated as model citizens in certain quarters of the Jewish population, we no longer can remain on the defensive.*[229]

To Hirsch, this was not like other delinquents who had deviated from faith and social morality, perhaps succumbing to the struggles of the ghetto. These were successful and professional gangsters who profited from white slaves and,

JEWS SMITE LEVEE TRAFFIC

Orthodox Leaders to Force Out White Slavers of the Race.

BITTER TOWARD THE FRANKS

Rabbis Weep as They Tell of Resort Keepers' Business.

The scourge of the orthodox Jews of Chicago through the rabbis and presidents of seventy congregations was laid yesterday upon the Frank brothers and other Jewish dwellers in the levee district and upon the Anshe Calvaria congregation, of which Julius Frank was the head, as well.

Just as the meeting of rabbis and presidents, which adopted drastic resolutions against the men of their race who were prospering from the money wrung from unfortunate women, was closing, the recalcitrant congregation by a unanimous vote elected Julius Frank to succeed himself as its president.

Frank declined the office and asked that Max Oppenheim, the vice president of the congregation, be named in his stead, and the suggestion was adopted unanimously. Then some of the members of the congregation said the public would declare Frank quit under fire and to show their faith in him they elected him superintendent of the cemetery.

But the gathering of Jewish churchmen at the Hebrew Institute in the evening did more than express its wrath against the conditions of the many of the race in the west side levee district. It named a permanent committee to plan and promote a campaign against vice which has for its object the driving out of every Jewish panderer from the city and the stripping of every honor from all men of their race who profit from white slavery.

in the case of Julius, held the highest administrative position in a synagogue. Marrying vice with public prominence was too much, and it was no wonder that Hirsch reiterated the shame the brothers caused the Jewish community four times in that single editorial. Similarly, Dr. Fishkin of the Chicago Hebrew Institute publicly condemned the Frank brothers, declaring that they were "a curse upon us," and demanded that Julius step down from his position as president.[230]

Yet words would not be enough. Hirsch called on all Jews to wage a civic war against white slavery and prostitution. Almost immediately, men who had long attended services at Anshe Kalvaria sought different synagogues, illustrating that the disgust permeated to all echelons of the Jewish community. Stirred by Hirsch's denunciations, Adolf Kraus and the B'nai B'rith order strengthened their crusade, which had begun a year earlier. With the help

This page and next two pages: A front-page headline following the meeting of Orthodox Jewish leaders, 1909. *From the* Chicago Tribune, *October 4, 1909.*

of other organizations—both Jewish and Christian—they helped to pledge $50,000 for Clifford Roe's work.[231] The slogan to their fervent movement would be: "Protect the girl!"[232] With this emphasis, several Jewish organizations strove to do just that. The Jewish Home for Girls, for example, provided lodging for homeless or immigrant girls to shelter them from potential harm or enslavement.[233] Moreover, simply discussing the issue served to educate the community and the parents of young girls. To be sure, one reason the Jews were so adamant in their response was because both ends of the vice deeply affected their community—the criminals and the victims.

The *Daily Jewish Press* commended Kraus and B'nai B'rith for their efforts to eradicate the "most shameful of all shameful businesses" in which "Jewish honor [was] at stake."[234] Once again, the newspaper defined the problem in terms of the shame it brought to the Jewish community. Like juvenile delinquency, the goal of all this action was to fix the impression of the Jews and the negative perceptions of the gentile community. Thus, they continued to mobilize.

First Step in Nation Wide War.

It is the first step in a nation wide campaign, say prominent Jews, to combat the white slave evil, which recent developments have shown to be increasing to an alarming extent among members of the race.

The committee will appeal to Mayor Busse today for detectives from the police department to work with private investigators to drive out more than 100 Jews in the west side levee engaged in the traffic of white slaves.

And the orthodox congregation of Ansha Calvaria is called upon in no uncertain terms to retract its action of adopting resolutions a few weeks ago upholding Julius Frank and his acts.

The plans of the Jewish churchmen go beyond mere regulation of the vice district in the west side. They will endeavor to uproot the entire levee district and drive it away from the west side neighborhood from which hundreds of young women have been lured by the nameless men the Jews now are seeking to drive out of the city or put in prison.

Dramatic Scene at Institute.

Chicago perhaps has never seen a more touching scene than that at the evening meeting of the Jewish churchmen. Gray-bearded rabbis shed tears as they talked in broken voices of the former glories of God's chosen people and the newest danger which is threatening that racial morality which has been the boast of the people for thousands of years. Earnest prayers to the God who led their fathers from an Egyptian task master to the chosen land of milk and honey were delivered amidst veritable choruses of amens.

And the Franks, a name which at first the speakers almost refused to pronounce, were flayed by almost every man present before the meeting ended. The Jewish press of the city also came in for a share of the scathing criticism, because speakers declared that the real truth about the Franks had been suppressed in the detailed accounts of the trial of Edward McCann, the police inspector, found guilty of bribe taking. It was declared that every Jew in the city should be told the truth concerning the business of the Franks in connection with levee resorts.

Jews Wronged Before the World.

"The revelations made at the McCann trial gave the world a wrong impression of the Jews and their morality as a race," declared B. Horwich, second vice president of the Hebrew Institute, in the meeting. "The world is apt to believe that the Jews condone such things. We must remove that false impression by condemning most emphatically those responsible for this disgrace.

"I have received letters from Jews out west telling me their existence is becoming intolerable. They are spurned by their neighbors because other people believe that all Jews are white slavers, for why otherwise would men in such a horrifying business be tolerated by a Jewish congregation. I have been asked in recent days if I was a member of that synagogue which has indorsed as its president a man who profits from white slaves."

S. B. Komaiko, secretary of the conference, asserted that Jewish honor must be preserved, saying:

"We must condemn this congregation for its indorsement of Julius Frank, and we must drive out the plague which is threatening the morality of members of our race."

Strikes at Synagogue's Honor.

Hyman Rosin, president of the Libawitz congregation, said:

"We must publicly cast out the filth from among us because as it is it is no longer an honor to be the president of any synagogue. Let us employ detectives, raise a fund, and prosecute these men who deal in women."

Rabbi Israelson said that not only was Julius Frank to be condemned, but all of those who sympathized with him. He advised the holding of massmeetings to condemn and drive out all Jews connected with white slavery.

The standing committee chosen to have complete charge of the campaign consists of Dr. David Blaustein, superintendent of the Hebrew Institute; Hyman Rosin, president of the Libawitz congregation, and M. Bordacow, president of the Vilna congregation.

On October 3, fourteen rabbis and seventy presidents of various congregations met at the Hebrew Institute. There, as the *Chicago Tribune* melodramatically recounted, "gray-bearded rabbis shed tears as they talked in broken voices of the former glories of God's chosen people."[235] Along with B'nai B'rith's efforts, the men established a permanent committee, headed by David Blaustein, to work toward wiping out every Jewish panderer.[236] They planned to earnestly request that Mayor Busse utilize both police detectives and private investigators in the hopes of removing what they believed to be more than one hundred Jews who participated in the white slave trade in the West Side levee. However, several speakers wished not to rely on "men who [were] politicians first" and instead argued, "Let us do this thing ourselves."[237] It is noteworthy that Jewish reformers consistently looked outside their community to bring change in spite of the opposition from other Jewish leaders. Perhaps they felt it was necessary. For one, this helped to emphasize that though the Jews were largely blamed for the trade, the problem of prostitution was societal. It diffused the blame by speaking to broader issues in American cities and demonstrated the Jewish community's commitment to municipal reform.

An unforeseen twist to the Frank brothers' story occurred near the meeting's close. The representatives of Anshe Kalvaria unanimously voted Julius Frank to succeed himself as the congregation's president. Frank rightly declined the offer. However, some members believed it best not to have Frank "quit under fire" and consequently elected him superintendent of its Jewish cemetery.[238] Both Louis and Julius Frank did swear they were out of the vice business for good and would join the crusade on the West Side. However, the congregation's move still came as a surprise. In response, the *Forward* indignantly asked, "What have the dead done to deserve such a disgrace?"[239] Dishonoring the living was bad enough, but disrespecting a person's ancestry was even worse. Yet more than anything, the Frank brothers taught the Chicago Jewry in 1909 that anyone could be part of the white slave trade and the underworld, including religious Jews. The problem was more extensive than anyone had imagined, and though the 1909 revelations excited more Jews to concentrate their efforts on eradicating the vice, the fight was far from over.

Throughout the second decade of the twentieth century, Chicagoans continued to learn the horrors of white slavery, and reformers struggled to clean up the levee. Jewish names filled the courtroom dockets, and community members strove to understand why. In 1910, anti-vice crusaders Clifford Roe and Ernest A. Bell both published and popularized white slavery narratives—sensationalized stories of sexual danger that frightened and engrossed the American public.[240] However, it is important to analyze, not simply accept, the degree of blame placed on the Jews by reformers. In his writings, Roe often stressed the relationship between criminality and foreignness, citing cases where defendants' surnames intimated French, Italian or Jewish origins.[241] Sociologist Brian Donovan argues that Roe was a nativist. Though he may have been hostile toward immigrants like the Eastern European Jews, Roe was more of an anti-Semite than a nativist. As

Portrait of anti-vice and white slave crusader Clifford Roe, 1908. *From the* Chicago Tribune, *July 26, 1908.*

scholars Edward Shapiro and David Gerber argue, anti-Semitism during the Progressive era was a separate phenomenon from nativism. Shapiro notes, "American anti-Semitism was part of a transnational mindset, not merely a response to American conditions."[242] Roe's perceived prejudice may signify that he unduly blamed the Jews for the white slave trade. If court records were not available, this would be an intriguing way in which to consider this history. Yet various investigator's reports and court records, including those kept by the Chicago Committee of Fifteen, are available, and under the names of numerous defendants, "Jew" appears.[243]

As white slave narratives increased public awareness of the vice, the push for reform on a federal level came in 1910. On June 25, Congress passed the Mann Act, also known as the White-Slave Traffic Act, which made it easier to prosecute procurers. In Chicago, Mayor Busse announced the establishment of the Vice Commission. In its 1911 report, the commission found the business of commercialized prostitution alive and well.[244] Furthermore, members observed that nearly all the victims were female immigrants from Eastern Europe.[245] Thus, not much had changed in spite of the reform efforts.

The city needed a fresh approach to dealing with the red-light district, and it came the following year. Prior to 1912, policemen and public officials had quelled the vice through the practice of "segregation." Under this policy, officials did not attempt to close all houses of ill repute but rather allowed some to exist in very particular and restricted districts, such as the Twenty-second Street district.[246] However, officials abandoned the toleration of vice after mounting protests from reformers, coupled with recommendations in 1911 from the Vice Commission in favor of suppression.[247] In turn, Mayor Harrison ordered the police department to close all resorts, and on October 2, 1912, the red-light district officially closed.[248] Nonetheless, this did not mean the end of the white slave trade.

Since the initial closing, the commercialized vice experienced an ebb and flow of activity coinciding with changes in the city's administration and the state's attorney's office.[249] In 1913, a state senate–appointed commission further investigated the white slave trade only to find the conditions of old. Girls associated with the city's brothels professed to the commission that nearly all proprietors of such establishments were Jewish. The *Daily Jewish Courier* lamented that the commission's finding made the "face of every respectable Jew blush with shame."[250] The writer concluded that the "growing generation" of Jews needed a better education in order to move away from the underworld into an "honorable place" in the city's social structure.[251] Recall that improving education was one of the three primary strategies to quell juvenile delinquency. The reporter's emphasis on the children rather than the criminals themselves suggests a certain degree of hopelessness with the current generation.

Yet the voice of the *Daily Jewish Courier* wavered in 1913. A July 23 article, in stark contrast to the March editorial, denied the *Chicago Tribune*'s accusations that houses of ill fame filled the ghetto district. The *Courier* fervently demanded that the chief of police, John McWeeny, investigate the neighborhood in order to "prove the falseness" of those claims.[252] In light of all the findings in the first decade of the twentieth century, this refutation sounds daft, but it does signify the mix of emotions that accompanies any negative charges against a people. In spite of this request, the social evil persisted. On July 18, 1922, the *Chicago Tribune* wrote an article entitled "The Return of White Slavery." Truthfully, the trafficking had never gone away. It seemed then that Chicagoans of the nineteenth century were right; prostitution was and would be an ineluctable part of American society—and a disgrace the Jews would have to bear well into the 1930s.[253]

Nevertheless, there is no mention of Louis or Julius Frank in Irving Cutler's seminal history, *The Jews of Chicago*. Nor is there reference to the Congregation Anshe Kalvaria, save its inclusion in a map of the Maxwell Street area. More surprising still is the absence of the Jewish community's connection to the prolific white slave trade of the early twentieth century and Chicago Jewry's struggle to combat the vice both for the sake of their daughters and their reputation in the city. However, Cutler is not alone in this oversight. It is truly an untold chapter in the history of Chicago's Jews that surprised my own grandmother, who grew up in the city. Fortunate curiosity led me to discover the Frank brothers from Herbert Asbury's brief inclusion of the McCann trial: "Wayman's last important act as State's Attorney was the prosecution of Police Inspector Edward McCann...on a charge of accepting bribes from brothel madams and saloon-keepers."[254] The *Chicago Tribune* archives illuminated the rest.

Why, then, has this been absent from the history of Jews in Chicago? Perhaps it was the way in which the community constructed its memory—a case of "historical amnesia" to help cope with a shameful association of the past.[255] Indeed, these were not the types of stories to impart to grandchildren while reminiscing about childhood memories on a Saturday morning. One way or another, the anecdotes fell into the background. Yet the Jewish community's relationship to the white slave trade is significant. Sometimes it is under adversity that one learns the most about a people and their true character. The actions of Jewish organizations and community members—prominent and nameless alike—demonstrated to the city that Jews would proactively respond to the appalling revelations of reformers. Moreover, it triggered a reevaluation of community goals and principles, forever shaping Chicago Jewry on the West Side.

5

POOLROOMS, FLASHLIGHTS AND GUNS

Jews in Gambling, 1890–1920

A special campaign, with flashlights and guns, is not necessary in the Jewish district.[256]
—the Daily Jewish Courier, *July 1914*

Years prior to the McCann trial, Julius and Louis Frank were saloonkeepers at Halsted and Madison Streets.[257] In addition to state senator John Broderick's bar, Frank Bros. was a popular establishment on the West Side near the turn of the century. Like several saloons of the time, it housed large gambling rooms that often attracted great crowds of players and spectators.[258] This was particularly true on Sunday, November 4, 1900. "The stud and draw poker tables," the *Chicago Tribune* recounted, "were crowded all afternoon and night" at the West Side saloon.[259] Rather than suppressing the open gaming, as was customary of late, police gave the "tiger freer rein" and put forth no effort to interfere.[260] It was, after all, two days before the country's presidential election, and that afternoon, a giant Democratic parade had filled the city's streets.[261] It was little surprise, then, that gaming at Frank Bros. went uninterrupted.

In Chicago, politicians utilized gambling as an instrument for raising campaign funds. As elections neared, gamblers, such as Julius and Louis Frank, pledged money to a politician or party in exchange for promised immunity from prosecution.[262] The *Chicago Tribune* noted that November 4 was one such instance: "Democratic politicians, anxious to cast a big vote for the Democratic ticket, pressed for funds for the campaign, have brought pressure to bear on the powers that be in the City Hall."[263] This was yet another example of the inextricable ties between politics and vice. That the newspaper specifically mentioned Frank Bros. and Senator Broderick's gambling house in its articles demonstrates the importance of these establishments to West Side gaming.

Even when the city did not tolerate the illicit activities at Frank Bros., the saloon and its proprietors continued to make the headlines. In an August 29, 1927 retrospective *Chicago Tribune* editorial, "From the Tribune's Columns," the paper shared events that had occurred on that day in history. Of the four stories chosen under "25 Years Ago Today," the following appeared: "CHICAGO.—Frank Bros.' gambling house, Halsted and Madison streets, was raided by detectives from Chief O'Neill's office, and fifty men were arrested."[264] Its curious inclusion in an article selective in nature further suggests the sizable reputation Frank Bros. had acquired throughout the city at the beginning of the twentieth century. Perhaps the brothers' saloon and, more broadly, Chicago's struggle with gambling were worth remembering.

Moreover, Julius and Louis Frank's involvement in gaming underscores the interconnectedness of all the underworld's vices and personalities. Therefore, while I am analyzing the Chicago Jewry's relationship to each immorality separately, it is vital to remember that all the criminal pursuits coexisted with and overlapped one another. That being said, the impact of prostitution and gambling on the Jewish community contrasted markedly and thus warrants separate consideration. The public's perception of the two vices, in part because of differences in reform efforts, helps to explain this variation.

Sociologist John Landesco rightly asserted, "Gambling as a pastime is less opprobrious than commercialized vice."[265] To many, gambling was less sensational, disgraceful and horrific in comparison to the white slave trade. There was no equivalent to the dramatic white slave narratives, which conjured up a very specific image of who the victims were—young and defenseless women, someone's daughter. Gambling's effects varied depending on the individual, and reformers never established such powerful imagery. Additionally, the effort to quell gambling was less concerted and public. No figure like Clifford Roe rose at the forefront of the movement, and no Jewish organization like B'nai B'rith pledged its support so fervently. Furthermore, reformers did not single out Jews as the root cause of gambling as they had for the white slave trade. In turn, its prevalence on the West Side did not elicit the same response from the Jewish community. Nevertheless, their participation in the gaming vice did reveal another layer in the struggle to define their identity and shape the community. With particular attention paid to both the career of Alderman Emanuel Abrahams and the *Chicago Tribune*'s attempted exposé of a West Side gambling house in the summer of 1913, the Jews in gambling illuminated the tensions between the *Chicago Tribune* and the *Daily Jewish Courier* or, broader still, the enmity between the Jewish community and the larger gentile population.

I

Gambling and the endeavor to suppress it were not new to the twentieth century. In 1830, the *Illinois Gazette* observed, "All the penal enactments against gaming have thus far been found ineffectual to arrest the evil."[266] While the state grappled with the growing iniquity, colonists and travelers continued to flood the booming settlement beside Lake Michigan. By Chicago's 1833 incorporation, this great concentration of inhabitants had facilitated horse race bets and card games to become a mainstay of the city.[267] Concurrently, early reformers, such as Reverend Jeremiah Porter, staged anti-gambling campaigns, but to little avail. It endured following the initial commercial boom, even when times turned sour. Despite the economic stagnation of Chicago in the 1840s, for example, the number of gambling houses continued to multiply.[268] Reformers and observers had no answer. In fact, an 1856 *Chicago Tribune* editorial mirrored the former sentiments of the *Illinois Gazette*, admitting, "This vice is hard to remedy."[269]

The second half of the nineteenth century saw an increase in the organization of the vice. Sociologist Frederick Thrasher's interview with an old resident of the city demonstrated that games of chance were popular activities among the earliest gangs of the nineteenth century, dating back to the 1860s.[270] On "Gamblers' Row"—an area on Clark Street that ran from Randolph to Monroe—gaming resorts supposedly were "clustered so thickly that there was room for no other business except a few saloons and an occasional brothel."[271] Individuals such as Mike McDonald took hold of the emerging bookmaking syndicate, beginning in the 1860s. He was a well-connected politician, card shark and close associate of Mayor Carter Harrison. McDonald was one of the mayor's chief advisers during his four consecutive terms in office, which began in 1879.[272] Significantly, Mayor Harrison's political platform allowed gambling houses to operate unmolested, and thus, McDonald rose to prominence. Chicago gamblers who flourished in the 1880s and 1890s did so by contributing to McDonald's "slush fund," which the gambler then distributed among various political allies, including Mayor Harrison—a familiar system of graft.[273] Following the mayor's assassination in 1893, McDonald's political influence diminished, and he retired from the vice to enjoy his vast and dishonest fortune.[274] His sudden departure illustrated that prominent gamblers waxed and waned with the changing of municipal administrations, as was true of the prostitution business.

With Mayor Harrison gone and the twentieth century on the horizon, the Civic Federation, a reform organization founded in 1893, worked tirelessly to suppress the city's gaming—"from the whirring roulette wheel to the lowly game of craps, from the faro layout to the policy traps."[275] Furthermore, the reformers sought to publicize the system of protection associated with gambling, which they concluded divvied up anywhere from $9,000 to $30,000 per month to municipal, county and state officials.[276] The Civic Federation, however, failed to influence Mayor John Hopkins, who believed certain resorts should remain in operation. In turn, the organization appointed a special subcommittee and hired a police force in order to raid several of the first-class gambling houses.[277]

Ensuing closures were only minor hindrances, and by the start of the twentieth century, gaming was back in full swing. On February 24, 1901, for example, the *Chicago Tribune* reported that 4,175 "policy" offices ran wide open in the city with approximately 146,000 plays made daily.[278] Policy, or the numbers game, was an illegal lottery that was particularly popular among poorer segments of the urban population since no ticket purchase was necessary. In policy shops, anyone could pick their three hopeful numbers, wagering from one cent to thirty dollars.[279] The article regretted the police department's general indifference but noted, "The only activity on the part of the police authorities occurred on Friday afternoon, when Captain Wheeler raided five 'shops' in the Ghetto district. He admitted that children from 8 to 9 years of age were playing and asserted that the game should be driven out of his district."[280]

With more than four thousand policy shops operating, the five raided in the Jewish district seem insignificant but proved that even the poorest segment of the population—the predominately Eastern European Jews—played the numbers game and that local police specifically targeted the district at a time when officers in other areas stood idly by. After all, policy required little capital and was a way to earn more with minimal time invested. In a community where fathers worked long hours to make ends meet, gambling was an attractive, albeit risky, auxiliary income. Perhaps proprietors of gambling dens recognized this economic desire of the Jewish population, thus choosing their locations to be around the ghetto district. The mention of children taking part in the gambling houses is also striking and no doubt added to the sensationalism of the article. Yet it affirmed that proprietors, such as Manny Abrahams, and some of the dens' young habitués were Jewish since the youth felt comfortable enough to hang out at such establishments.[281] Perhaps they saw their older brothers or familiar faces from the Maxwell Street market. The nature of the ghetto would not exclude such possibilities. What is more, it speaks to the conditions of the ghetto and the realities of tenement living, which, as we have seen, often resulted in minimal parental supervision and subsequent juvenile delinquency. This was especially true for Chicago Jewry at a time when many critical communal centers, like the Chicago Hebrew Institute that emphasized morality and education of the Eastern European immigrants, did not yet exist.[282]

Mayor Carter Harrison Jr., in a 1903 interview with the *Chicago Tribune*, discussed his administration's approach to gambling and his overall desire to clean up the city's government. He believed in the regulation, not the suppression, of gaming since it was "one of the oldest and most universal passions of men" and not easily remedied.[283] Harrison shaped the problem of gambling around the question of personal liberty, maintaining that many viewed gambling as a right. In turn, he allowed certain card games to operate in clubs supposedly for members only. Nonetheless, the mayor recognized the difficulties of effectively employing this strategy for a vice that touched all segments of the population, including the most poverty-stricken. He observed, "One curious phase of gambling in Chicago is afforded by the Russian Jews on the west side. It illustrates the universal desire of those people who can least afford to lose money in this way risking their small amounts with absolute recklessness."[284]

There are several curiosities embedded in the above observation. It revealed that even the city's mayor believed that Russian Jews were the poorest of all Chicagoans. This is significant because the *Chicago Tribune* transmitted Harrison's view to the greater public and, to a certain extent, unquestionably shaped their view of the Jewish community. Additionally, his identification of the Jews living on the West Side as solely Russian evinces the mayor and perhaps the city's oversimplification and ignorance of the ghetto. Although a large majority of its inhabitants were Russian by 1903, it is worth noting that emigrants from various parts of Europe lived on the West Side, including Jews from Poland, Lithuania and Latvia. Moreover, Mayor Harrison's use of the word "recklessness" when describing the Jews' gambling behavior suggests that their participation

Two-time mayor of Chicago Carter Henry Harrison Jr. (front right) standing on a city sidewalk beside Alderman Thomas Carey (front left), Chicago, 1906. *Chicago History Museum, DN-0003896.*

was serious and perhaps widespread. Though the mayor could not justify the impoverished Jews' relationship to gambling, I believe it truly was an avenue for excitement and economic mobility in a community where such opportunity was rather limited.

Concurrently, the gaming business in Chicago came under the control of three principal syndicates in the wake of Michael McDonald's departure from the vice. There was Mont Tennes, James O'Leary and Alderman Johnnie Rogers—the gambling bosses on the North, South and West Sides, respectively.[285] In the Loop district, the control of handbooks and games primarily rested with Aldermen Kenna and Coughlin of the First Ward, as well as gambler Tom McGinnis. It was in the downtown district that the rival factions collided with one another and sought to invade, leading to the bombing war of 1907.[286] The *Chicago Tribune*, in an article relating a failed attempt to blow up Mont Tennes's residence, wrote, "The whole series of incidents grows out of jealousy between warring factions of gamblers and of efforts on the part of partisans of the opposition to fright the men thus attacked."[287] As warring subsided, new district rulers, though not as prominent as Tennes, emerged in the coming years, including Manny Abrahams.

Emanuel "Manny" Abrahams was born to a Chicago Jewish family on July 7, 1866, and raised in the Maxwell Street district.[288] His community eventually helped to elect him to the state's House of Representatives in November 1906.[289] Four years later, in the 1910 aldermanic election, Abrahams made the Democratic ticket as candidate for the Ninth Ward. The *Daily Jewish Courier* implored its readership to vote for Abrahams, stating, "The Jewish public knows…he was always willing to aid a Jew. Emanuel Abrahams as Alderman will rightly represent the ninth ward. The voters will then have an alderman whom they can justly be proud of."[290] Similarly, community member Ben Levy called Abrahams "a man of character and energy."[291] However, the revered and soon-to-be alderman also operated a gambling resort at 451 South Halsted Street. While he insisted that his brother owned the saloon, this pretense existed only in name. In fact, investigators found that the Maxwell Street Police Station protected Manny's gambling resort, which allowed him to conduct gaming with no punishment.[292] The duality of Manny Abrahams's persona as both a politician and saloonkeeper certainly complicated his image and calls the *Courier*'s praise of him into question. After Abrahams's election to the city council in 1910, findings by the Civil Service Commission deepened this rift in personality.

In September 1911, the Civil Service Commission began its investigation into the established system of political graft associated with gambling, city officials and the police force. The move came after charges of bribery had surfaced following a day of open gambling outside Comiskey Park, where the Labor Day Gotch-Hackenschmidt wrestling match took place.[293] Facts presented to the commission revealed that "Hinky Dink" Kenna, James Quinn and Barney Brogan were the big bosses of vice districts where gambling flourished without police intervention.[294] Yet informants for the commission soon named three additional politicians, who, though not as important as the Kenna-Quinn-Grogan triumvirate, were still powerful in their respective districts, particularly in handling the affairs of police-protected gambling.[295]

On September 16, the *Chicago Tribune*'s front-page article first exposed the names of these three politicians, one of whom was Jewish alderman Manny Abrahams. Two months later, the sworn testimony of former bookmaker Ben

Hyman to the Civil Service Commission corroborated the involvement of Abrahams in the graft-collecting machine. According to the *Chicago Tribune*'s summation, Hyman described Manny Abrahams in the following manner: "Former [state] representative; controls the places operated by the 'orthodox Jews in the Maxwell street district.'"[296] Hyman's testimony not only gave credence to Abrahams's ties to vice but also indicated rather precisely that Eastern European Jews, who composed the Orthodox community, owned several gambling resorts in the ghetto.

However, the Civil Service Commission never filed suit against Abrahams, and its investigation, other than discharging a handful of police officials, failed to curb the city's gaming enterprise.[297] Instead, Emanuel Abrahams continued to serve as boss of the Jewish ghetto until his sudden passing on July 1, 1913. He died after speaking before the council judiciary committee in favor of an amendment to the ordinance, which banned his peddler constituency from shouting their services and products on the streets.[298] In other words, Manny Abrahams died representing his Jewish constituency, just as they knew he would back on the eve of the 1910 aldermanic election. His legacy seemed to vary then depending on whom one asked. In the eyes of the Chicago Jewry, he was a figure to be proud of who gave the Jewish community the political representation they deserved. As a matter of fact, in the Chicago Foreign Language Press Survey's twelve volumes of translated articles from the leading Jewish newspapers, not one denounced Emanuel Abrahams. That is not to say that such an article did not exist, but its exclusion from the volumes is in itself extremely telling. Moreover, at his funeral, the *Chicago Tribune* reported, "more than 10,000 persons [including 'Hinky Dink' Kenna], from riff-raff to highbrow, filed down the aisles to view the body," which suggests the wide-reaching appeal of the alderman.[299] Others, however, would remember Manny Abrahams quite differently. To them, he was the vice lord of the Maxwell Street district who functioned prominently within the city's gambling, graft-collecting machine of the early twentieth century.

II

Just two weeks after Manny Abrahams's passing, the *Chicago Tribune* further exposed the gambling in the Maxwell Street district in what became a controversial nighttime investigation and shooting. In its wake, there was a brief newspaper war between the *Chicago Tribune* and the *Daily Jewish Courier*. In the following analysis, the intention is not to decide which story—the *Chicago Tribune*'s or the *Courier*'s—was most accurate but rather to understand why the accounts varied, how the newspapers spoke to each other and what this illustrated in relation to the Chicago Jewish community.

Just who made the telephone call that prompted the *Chicago Tribune*'s initial investigation into a West Side establishment is unclear. According to its July 14, 1913 article, on the evening of Saturday, July 12, a woman phoned the newspaper's office to complain that her son was wasting the family's wages away at the 813 West Maxwell Street gambling house.[300] However, the *Chicago Tribune* reported on the fifteenth that it was the father who called—upset that his son had been "dropping into those Maxwell Street gambling houses."[301] Nevertheless, in response to the complaint, the newspaper sent a reporter to 813 West Maxwell Street—in the heart of the ghetto—to investigate about 9:00 p.m. The journalist estimated that 150 gamblers played stuss and craps and crowded the saloon's three rooms. Given the establishment's location, it is not surprising that gamblers played stuss, or "Jewish faro"—possibly from the Yiddish *shtos* or *stos*. It was a variation of the card game faro, developed by gangsters on the Lower East Side of New York about 1885.[302] The correspondent advised the *Chicago Tribune* to photograph the conditions as proof of the wide-open betting, and the newspaper took the reporter's recommendation.[303] At 11:45 p.m., circulation manager Max Annenberg, a *Tribune* photographer and three other employees arrived again at 813 West Maxwell Street.

Bear in mind, I extracted the words and phrases in quotations that follow directly from the *Chicago Tribune*'s July 14 article to illustrate how the newspaper framed its recollection of the incident. The photographer took a "flash light photograph" through an open window of one of the gambling rooms. Upon seeing the flash, the forty or so gamers fled the room, making a "concerted attack" as the *Tribune* employees retreated to their automobile. The gamblers, "who had developed the proportions of a mob," threatened the newspapermen, and several of the saloon's frequenters "brandished revolvers." One such gambler fired a shot at the employees, and to "scare back the wildly shouting crowd," Max Annenberg shot one bullet in return "from the only revolver they [the newspapermen] had." The bullet found Alexander Belford, a twenty-three-year-old Russian Jew, in the chest. He lived at 1304 Newberry Avenue—a mere 220 feet away from 813 West Maxwell Street—which demonstrated how gambling dens and homes suffocated one another in the Jewish ghetto.[304] As the employees drove off, "there was a fusillade of bullets aimed in the direction of the automobile." In the early morning of July 13, the county hospital admitted Belford and stated his condition was favorable, thus ending the night's physical altercation.[305]

There is a very distinct way in which the *Chicago Tribune* framed the disastrous exposé, apparent in the language utilized in this July 14 article. The reporter consistently positioned the gamblers as angry and aggressive. Additionally, the article never referred to Alexander Belford as a victim. On the contrary, the writer painted the *Tribune* employees as victims—the reactive party. In particular, one reads Max Annenberg as highly reluctant to fire the gun, even in the face of a mob with many revolvers. This no doubt shaped the general public's opinion of the incident and of the establishment in the Jewish community. Few Chicagoans could read the articles in the Yiddish *Daily Jewish Courier*, and exposure to a Jewish perspective came only from carefully selected columns, included in the *Chicago Tribune* and translated by its employees. Before placing the *Daily Jewish Courier* in dialogue with the *Tribune*, the history of 813 West Maxwell Street and the general effect the exposé had on vice is necessary.

Frank Larman, also spelled "Lehrman," and his partner, Philip Stubbinski, were the proprietors of the Maxwell Street gambling den.[306] Though nothing is known of their individual backgrounds, it is apparent that their gambling house was notorious. In the month or so leading up to the shooting, the Maxwell Street police had raided the establishment thrice, fined the owners and sent three gamblers to Bridewell.[307] Captain Storen, recently transferred to the Maxwell Street station, told the *Tribune* that Detectives Roth and Weisbaum, both Jews, made daily visits to the "dump" and believed "he [Larman] ought not to be allowed to run any kind of a place—not even a coffee house."[308] The difficulties inherent in suppressing the gaming at 813 West Maxwell Street lay in Larman and Stubbinksi's political backing—first from Manny Abrahams and then from his brother and successor, Morrie Abrahams. Shortly after raids occurred, political friends of the proprietors always appeared with bonds for their release.[309] Letters to the *Tribune* from concerned wives, mothers and children of the gamblers, similar to the phone call on July 12, exacerbated the police's frustrations.[310]

Yet the July 13 exposé elicited a greater response from the underworld and the city's government than the previous three raids on 813 West Maxwell Street. In the *Chicago Tribune*'s July 15 cover story, "Clamp Lid Tight on Gambling Dens," the newspaper declared, "To all parts of the town the word went out to close up and the gamblers obeyed. They were told to lie low until the effects of the clash of Saturday night should subside." It is impossible to know whether the reporter embellished the statement to further justify the *Tribune*'s controversial actions, thus clearing its name, or if the comment truly reflected the realities of the underworld. Regardless, the article's position on the front page in itself reveals the importance the *Tribune* believed this incident demanded and the vast number of people who would read or see the story. Additionally, the journalist claimed there were at least five gambling dens easily found in the vicinity of Maxwell and Halsted Streets.[311] However, since there is no comparison to vice located in the rest of the city's districts, the assertion puts the Jewish ghetto in a rather negative light. The next day's *Chicago Tribune* was no different—"Revokes License of Gambling Den" graced the newspaper's front page. It related that Mayor Harrison Jr. had revoked Frank Larman's license at 813 West Maxwell Street. The mayor chose to take action because Larman permitted open gambling and repeatedly violated police regulations.[312]

The closing of the saloon did not signify the end of the affair. Not only was Max Annenberg's trial for assault with a deadly weapon pending, but also the *Daily Jewish Courier* responded to the *Tribune*. The *Courier*'s history, as well as its function in the community, exemplifies why its perspectives are fairly representative of Jews in the ghetto and thus critical to explore. Located at 1214 South Halsted Street, a tenth of a mile from Larman's saloon, the *Daily Jewish Courier* was an independent Yiddish paper established in 1887 by a Russian immigrant.[313] In this sense, the *Courier* was truly a product of the Eastern European wave of immigration into the Maxwell Street ghetto. The paper was Orthodox-oriented, as was its audience—the predominantly Russian Jewry. The *Courier* greatly influenced the Jewish immigrants, historian Irving Cutler notes, by "shaping political viewpoints, arbitrating domestic situations...and giving a basic education in Americanization."[314] In turn, its editorials concerning the shooting of Alexander Belford—which served to express the opinion of the newspaper—reflect the perspective of the Jewish community.

The *Courier*'s writers discussed the exposé in language that was distinct from that of the *Tribune*. A passage from a July 23 editorial illustrates this contrast best. The *Courier*'s writer reported:

> *As is already known, the* Chicago Tribune, *after its employee shot and seriously wounded the Jewish young man, Alexander Belford,*

created a rumpus, to the effect that the Jewish Ghetto is contaminated with gambling houses…and instead of helping to bring its employee, who shot an innocent young man, to the law, it intended to avert the public opinion from the gun battle, by creating sensational stories of indecency prevailing in the Jewish district.[315]

By linking Max Annenberg's actions directly to Alexander Belford's critical condition, the *Courier* underscored the culpability of the *Tribune* employee—the incident's instigator. This differed greatly from the *Tribune*'s account, which downplayed both the shooting and Belford's injury, ensuring that Annenberg had acted in self-defense. The *Courier* also contended that the *Tribune* was diverting attention away from the true headline—Annenberg's shooting of an innocent Jew—by its creation of "sensational" stories of vice on the West Side. Implicit in this assertion is that these stories were exaggerations of the truth. From the *Courier*'s perspective, the *Tribune* broadcasted an unfair and distorted view of the Jewish community to the city and had done so repeatedly since the community formed. Out of this affair, the *Tribune* charged that the Jewish ghetto was full of brothels and crooked gambling houses. To this, the *Courier* replied, "This accusation is false, as are all other accusations made by the *Tribune* against the Jewish district."[316] It was clear that this tension between the *Tribune* and *Courier* went far beyond the shooting of Alexander Belford. In truth, it reflected the Jewish community's struggles to defend its pride and identity.

On July 17, the *Daily Jewish Courier* featured an editorial entitled "There Is No Harm in Telling the Truth." Alongside addressing the gambling exposé, the author gave thought to the *Tribune*'s verbal attacks on the ghetto district and the Jewish community's relationship to vice. The *Courier* maintained that the *Tribune* was wrong for not considering the bygone days of the West Side residents and grounded its defense in the historical context of these Russian immigrants. By writing in first-person plural, the newspaper appeared to speak for the entire community. "It will naturally take time," the columnist proclaimed, "before we live up to our ancient standard [of morality]. The effect of thousands of years of inquisitions, and treacherous pogroms [in Russia], cannot change us over night."[317] Indeed the Chicago Russian Jewish community came from a country where Jews knew "no conception of citizenship" and "did not even have the so-called right of living."[318] The editorial illuminated the transition these immigrants continued to go through in adapting to American life yet also emphasized the progress made thus far. The Jewish community had developed institutions and cared for its elderly, sickly and poverty-stricken neighbors with "no one to thank but its own members…who always received the greatest support from the *Jewish Courier*."[319] The newspaper believed the *Tribune* focused too heavily on the shameful rather than the admirable work of the Jewish community. This, in turn, hindered the Jew's path to further moral progress by constantly forcing the community to reevaluate itself. "It [*Chicago Tribune*] attempted, through its columns," the *Courier* reflected, "to place us in such light that we often wondered how low we had fallen."[320]

That being said, the *Courier* did not deny the existence of some gambling in the Maxwell Street district but wished to share the other side of the story— the community's competency to reform—that the *Tribune* failed to include. "It is true that gambling goes on on the Jewish West Side," the *Courier* noted in its July 17 editorial.

> *Gambling and indecency is being suppressed…through the tireless efforts of the* Daily Jewish Courier, *through the activities of the Chicago Hebrew Institute, the Maxwell Street Settlement, the social clubs, the Joseph Medill School and through other such organizations which are filling up the Jewish district so rapidly that soon there will be no room for these pool rooms and night restaurants.*[321]

The editorial's emphasis on the community's own reform institutions suggests that Jews did not need the *Tribune*, or the gentile community, to meddle in their affairs. Rather, it seemed to insist on the independence of the Chicago Jewry in guiding the community. Of course, from Clifford Roe's role in the crusade to end white slavery, we know this was not entirely true. Nonetheless, it is significant that Chicago Jews saw themselves as a self-reliant people and encouraged the *Tribune* to take greater note of its achievements. The editorial concluded, "If the *Tribune* wishes to extend a helping hand in this good work…let [them] take pictures of the accomplishments of…the Federated Jewish Orthodox Charities and of all other institutions where children are taught to be good citizens, good men and good Jews."[322]

There was yet another interesting aspect of the dialogue between the *Chicago Tribune* and the *Daily Jewish Courier* in light of the Maxwell Street gambling affair. It concerned the *Tribune*'s use of excerpts from the *Jewish Daily Press* and the *Jewish Record*, translated from Yiddish to English, to demonstrate the disgust felt by the Jewish community after revelations of gambling on the West Side. In fact, on July 20, the *Tribune* included an entire editorial from the July 17 edition of the *Jewish Daily Press* entitled,

"The Gamblers and Their Friends."[323] In the column, the *Daily Press* attacked the *Jewish Courier*, asserting that it was the organ of the gamblers. "The *Jewish Courier* wanted nothing less than to turn this into a 'Jewish case.' It represented it so as if it were a case of an anti-Semitic reporter making a raid upon innocent 'green Jews.'"[324] The *Tribune*'s translation of the editorial served to discredit the *Courier* and, in doing so, made the actions of the *Tribune* appear more righteous.

Of course, the *Courier* criticized the accuracy of these translations. After the inclusion of a statement from the *Courier*, its contributor condescendingly wrote, "We, in the office of the *Courier*, understand the language in which the *Tribune* is written, and in the office of the *Tribune* they must rely upon some lad whenever they want to know what the *Courier* writes."[325] This unquestionably complicates the reading of the newspapers. Yet deciphering whether the *Jewish Daily Press* actually wrote what the *Tribune* translated is less important than to consider why the *Tribune* continued to belabor the existence of West Side gambling in its columns and to tarnish the perception of the Jewish community, even when the claims were irrelevant to the innocence of Max Annenberg. Surely the vice was just as prevalent throughout the rest of Chicago. One possibility is that the *Tribune* was truthfully trying to root out the city's vices and felt that the investigation into 813 West Maxwell Street presented the perfect opportunity to concentrate its efforts on the West Side. When the situation went awry, the employees had to further justify their actions and their importance to municipal reform, thus emphasizing that periodicals like the *Jewish Daily Press* welcomed the exposé.[326] However, it is equally possible that the *Tribune* sought to isolate the West Side community, voice an anti-Semitic perspective and depict its Russian Jewish immigrants as a burden the city had to bear.

Nearly three months after the flashlight photography and gun battle at Frank Larman's poolroom, a jury in Judge Brentano's court acquitted Max Annenberg of any criminal activity in the shooting of Jewish gambler Alexander Belford.[327] The jury found that Annenberg fired the shot in self-defense, accepting the *Tribune*'s account of the night's events. In truth, though, the verdict is insignificant. The written war between the *Chicago Tribune* and the *Daily Jewish Courier*—the Chicago citizenry and the Jewish community—remained.

The episode reveals that crime truly offers a unique look into the formation of the Chicago Jewry, as it forced community members to make sense of who they were and where they stood in the eyes of the public. The media attention surrounding alderman Manny Abrahams and various Jewish gamblers, as well as subsequent police raids, did not, of course, mark the end of the vice on the West Side. Indeed, a private investigator wrote of the same "Abrahams's saloon" at 921 West Twelfth Street in an August 5, 1914 report, presumably owned at that time by his brother Morrie. While the informant watched men play card games, he observed, "They all looked like Jew business men to me."[328] Furthermore, another report from December 2, 1914, noted that at Abrahams's saloon, "Frank Lehrman" was there among other gamblers.[329] Such were the cyclical workings of the Chicago underworld and the West Side gangsters.

6

THE FLY-BY-NIGHT JEWS

Bootleggers and Racketeers, 1915–1935

The Friends of prohibition claimed that when we eliminated the manufacture and sale of liquor, crime would disappear. The truth is, however, that since prohibition has been introduced, the number of criminals and crimes has increased.[330]
—*Dr. S.M. Melamed, April 1923*

As 1920 approached, changing national and local circumstances helped to usher in a new era of crime and challenges for the Chicago Jewish community. To be sure, their involvement in prostitution and gambling persisted, but two new avenues of vice took center stage on the West Side: bootlegging and labor racketeering. They encompass a single chapter because they were more or less concurrent movements in the city's culture of crime critical to the understanding of the Chicago Jewry. The passing of the Volstead Act led to a great increase in organized crime throughout the country during the 1920s. In Chicago, rival gangsters waged war against one another for control of the beer market in various territories, resulting in countless murders. On the city's West Side, there was one such beer war between the Klondike O'Donnell brothers and Al Capone—the latter emerging as the kingpin of the city's bootleggers and rising to national prominence.[331] Within these feuds, Jews played important roles, including Julian "Potatoes" Kaufman and Bummie Goldstein.[332] While the stories of these Jewish gangsters and the beer wars are fascinating, they are not the focus of this chapter because they did not directly interact with or impact Chicago Jewry. Additionally, we do not learn much about the community through the actions of these Jewish gangsters.

Instead, the Chicago Jewish community's relationship to Prohibition will concentrate on the abuse and bootlegging of sacramental wine that proliferated in the 1920s. Scholars, such as Hannah Sprecher and Jenna Weissman Joselit, have chronicled this scandal in New York, but they have paid little attention to the larger racket in Chicago, where in 1924, the "withdrawals of wine for sacramental use exceeded those of any other community in the country and were far in excess of the sacramental wine consumption before prohibition."[333] Thus, this disparity is significant and warrants further investigation. The bootlegging was largely attributable to Orthodox Jews and their religious leaders due to the subgroup's economic position, as well as their greater adherence to prescribed religious rituals. However, bootlegging did affect the entire Jewish community—not simply the inhabitants of the ghetto—and spotlighted the stark contrasts present between Chicago's German Reform and Eastern European Orthodox Jewry.

While articles in a variety of English and Yiddish newspapers continued to recount the Jewish brand of bootlegging in Chicago during the 1920s, others related the rise of labor grafting, or racketeering, on the West Side. "Talk to any local racketeer," a November 27, 1927 column in the *Chicago Tribune* offered, "and he will immediately inform you that Chicago is the haven city for the racketeers of the country."[334] Sociologist John Landesco defines racketeering as the "exploitation for personal profit, by means of violence, of a business association or employees' organization."[335] These associations—distinct from the legitimate Chicago trade unions—enforced their laws and price regulations through intimidation, bombings, assaults and shootings.[336] The same *Tribune* report declared that the Jewish residents on the West Side were the "hardest hit" by the workings of racketeers, most apparent in the kosher food trades.

This phenomenon, which pitted Jew against Jew, greatly shaped the economy and labor movement of the West Side community from around 1916 to the early 1930s because the racketeers' harsh regulations impacted goods that Orthodox Jews relied on: kosher food. Together, then, bootlegging and labor racketeering were highly disruptive to the Jewish community because they invaded both the synagogue and marketplace—two of the three places central to the culture of Eastern European Jews and, thus, the ghetto's denizens.[337] Furthermore, the vices underscored the religious and economic differences between Orthodox and Reform Jews and presented both a moral and dishonest face of the Orthodox rabbis, which reflected the increasing organization of the Chicago rabbinate, the complexities of the Eastern European Jewish experience and the further development of the West Side community.

I

During the consideration of the National Prohibition Act in 1919, which sought to ban the "manufacture, sale or transportation of intoxicating liquors," Orthodox Jews and Catholic clergymen alike lobbied for the allowance of wine for sacramental purposes.[338] Prohibition, they argued, would undermine the freedom of religion under the First Amendment since the use of wine was central to several of their customs and rituals. For example, the Judaic religion requires a Conservative or Orthodox rabbi to use wine "for Kiddush [blessing over the wine] on Sabbaths and holiday eves, for Habdalah on Saturday nights and particularly so on wedding and circumcision occasions, and at the Passover Seder table."[339] That Kiddush and Habdalah were weekly rituals demonstrates the stakes of Prohibition to observant Jews.

In order to secure the bill's passage, drafters of the Volstead Act compromised by allowing for the sacramental use of alcohol under Section 6 of the amendment.[340] It entailed a system in which the "head of any conference or diocese or other ecclesiastical jurisdiction may designate any rabbi, minister, or priest to supervise the manufacture of wine to be used for the purposes and rites in this section mentioned, and the person designated may, in the discretion of the Commissioner, be granted a permit to supervise such manufacture."[341] The bill passed on January 16, 1919, and a year later, the Eighteenth Amendment to the U.S. Constitution went into effect. The time in between was spent, in part, formulating the rules and regulations for the manufacture of kosher wine, and the Internal Revenue Department (IRD) employed several rabbis to help in this process.[342]

Yet Jews in Chicago and across the nation were still uncertain of how the system would operate, even after the Prohibition era began. With Passover on the horizon, the *Sunday Jewish Courier* expressed such confusion in February 1920: "Some state that the rabbi issues the permit to the wine dealer and the latter delivers the wine to the member [of the congregation]; others say that only the rabbi can handle the wine, but he can give it away or sell it."[343] The following month, the system grew clearer. The *Chicago Tribune* explained that each Jewish family could get ten gallons of wine yearly. Each family would receive this allotment through the rabbi of their congregation, who would be responsible for its distribution. The IRD was set to circulate forms to the rabbis of congregations in March 1920. Each rabbi then used the form to record how many families were in their respective congregations and what quantity of wine they required. In return, rabbis received withdrawal permits from the government. Since families could also make their own wine for sacramental purposes, several rabbis decided to designate committees on distribution to determine whether and how much families intended to purchase wine through the synagogue.[344]

However, this system of sacramental wine allocation was prone to abuse, particularly in Orthodox Jewish communities like the Maxwell Street settlement. While Protestant ministers and Catholic priests were controlled and disciplined by their bishops, rabbis did not have such supervision, as the Judaic faith lacked the organization and hierarchy of Christianity.[345] It was thus harder to monitor the integrity of every rabbi. Additionally, the government had difficulty confirming the validity of rabbinic credentials because the majority of Orthodox rabbis were recent immigrants from Eastern Europe.[346] Herbert Asbury also observed, "Anyone could become a rabbi upon being certified by a senior rabbi, and the senior rabbis were gentle, unsuspicious old men with an abiding faith in the goodness of humanity and easily imposed upon."[347] His depiction is an oversimplification of the process and an unfair caricature of the religious leaders, but it does suggest the ease with which corruption could and did occur. This potential for scandal became even greater the following year—in 1922—when the federal government lifted several of the more stringent constraints placed on the issuance of sacramental wine. It came after a series of hearings between members of the IRD and various religious ministers who complained of the difficulties in securing an adequate quantity and quality of wine. Consequently, the IRD removed the limit on the amount of sacramental wine a rabbi or priest could obtain, except when it was intended for home use, as was sometimes the case for Jewish families.[348] This move, of course, made the law easier to circumvent.

Naturally, since the beginning of Prohibition, some Orthodox rabbis in Chicago did just that, but the media reported very little about the growing misconduct. That is, until Julius Rosenwald formally spoke out against sacramental wine and its abuse among rabbis at the Golden Jubilee convention of the Union of American Hebrew Congregations at Hotel Astor in New York on January 24, 1923.[349] Rosenwald was a Reform Jew and the son of German

Photograph of Julius Rosenwald standing in a train station, Chicago, 1926.
Chicago History Museum, DN-0082131, Chicago Daily News, Inc.

immigrants, born in Springfield, Illinois, in 1862. One year after speaking at the convention, he would become president and chairman of the board of Sears, Roebuck and Company. While reaching great prominence in the business world, Rosenwald was always very philanthropic and concerned about the state of the Jewish community.[350] It certainly is not surprising that he was the one to publicize the scandal on a national scale.

Before members of the American Hebrew Congregations, Julius Rosenwald urged the organization to call for an end to the sacramental wine privilege for Jewish rabbis and synagogues.[351] He believed both Orthodox and Reform rabbis were in accord that wine was not necessary for religious rites, and instead, grape juice could be used. "Nevertheless," Rosenwald lamented, "there are known to be certain men who, under the guise of religion, have misused the privilege granted by congress and have made a business of selling wine permits contrary to the intent of the law."[352] Regardless of whether it was a limited or widespread practice, Rosenwald dared, "If these offenders operate in the name of religion we should accept this challenge to our self-respect."[353] As was the case with denunciations directed toward Jews in other criminal pursuits, Rosenwald framed the illicit selling of wine around its assault on the pride and character of his people. Jews must take action in order to "prevent a disgraceful situation."[354] His choice of words intimated and reinforced that the reputation of both Jews and Judaism was of critical importance to the community. Though he primarily spoke to unite all Jews behind his cause, at one point, Rosenwald strikingly singled out the Eastern European immigrants. He observed, "They cannot, because of sheer force of weight and crowding in cities, adjust themselves as quickly as did their more widely dispersed brethren of a former day [the wave of German immigrants]. As a result, we have many new Jewish problems."[355] Implicit in this accusation, which transcended far beyond the abuse of sacramental wine, was his criticism of Orthodox Jews, overwhelmingly from Eastern Europe, and the troubles they imposed on the Jewish community.

On a local and national stage, Rosenwald's stance on sacramental wine and his speech in New York elicited a negative response from Orthodox Jewry. In Chicago's *Sunday Jewish Courier*, Dr. Melamed, a prominent Yiddish writer, remarked, "I have the greatest respect for Mr. Rosenwald, but I cannot recognize him as an authority on questions of Jewish religion. Whether the Jewish religion requires genuine wine or grape juice for Kiddush and Habdalah is a matter which only the Orthodox rabbis can decide."[356] Owing to Rosenwald's success and stature in Chicago, it is significant that Dr. Melamed was so frank in dismissing his recommendation, especially in light of a crime associated with the use of wine. In doing so, Dr. Melamed discredited Reform Judaism and argued that all authority on religious matters rested in the hands of Orthodox rabbis. On February 1, Rabbi Gabriel Wolf Margolis, president of the Assembly of Hebrew Orthodox Rabbis based in New York, echoed the sentiments of Dr. Melamed. "Mr.

Rosenwald…is not an authority on religious matters. Their [reform rabbis] opinion as to the obligation to use sacramental wine should not have great weight."[357] Though there may have been Orthodox Jews who differed, these testimonies came from individuals of high esteem and likely reflected the dominant perspective.

Rosenwald's speech and the reaction to it illuminated the deep divisions that had developed between the Orthodox and Reform Jewry in Chicago, evident in articles found in the West Side newspapers during the 1920s. In September 1921, for example, the *Daily Jewish Courier* received a letter from an individual who complained bitterly about the paper's opposition to Reform Judaism. In response, the *Courier*'s writer asserted, "We repeat once more that American Reform Judaism is the biggest fraud of the Jewish religion…an internal enemy with which we never can make peace."[358] In a 1922 article, Baruch Sholom Levy described the Reform Jews as the "assimilators…who aren't particularly interested in Judaism."[359] It appeared, then, that the Orthodox resented the Reform because they had abandoned traditional features of the religion and, in turn, had secured more social and economic mobility than the largely impoverished, unassimilated Eastern European Jews on the West Side. Perhaps Orthodox rabbis' insistence on using sacramental wine, then, was both an assertion of authority over Reform Jews and an economic opportunity. Many Orthodox rabbis could profit from the illicit wine transactions and supplement their wages, which were "one-third of the salaries the Reform rabbis get."[360]

In spite of Julius Rosenwald's speech in January 1923, the resolution to eliminate sacramental wine did not materialize. On the contrary, 1923 saw a vast increase in the sale of sacramental wine in Chicago, and permits for withdrawals totaled 1,200,000 gallons—400,000 more than in the larger metropolis of New York.[361] According to the 1920 U.S. census, New York City's population was 853,165, while Chicago's was 516,422.[362] Arrests grew frequent, and the workings of this graft ring became clearer after investigations in 1924. In some cases, rabbis sold the permits to wine distributors, who then sold it at a higher price to the wine merchants.[363] Agents also found permits issued to congregations that had already closed or that never existed. Upon reviewing several congregation member lists, agents discovered that they carried the names of "nearly every Jew who had died in Chicago in thirty years."[364] In October, federal officers "dashed out into the ghetto" to arrest David Wexler, who was a middleman between the wine bootleggers and the "alleged crooked members" of the Prohibition enforcement.[365] Each new finding made Jewish involvement more shameful, and by the end of the month, federal grand jurors had indicted a total of 53 people connected with the sacramental wine racket.[366]

On July 23, 1925, this list expanded to include Major Percy B. Owen, federal Prohibition director for Illinois, and his predecessor, Ralph W. Stone. Federal investigators had traced graft money directly to Owen's office, and the two allegedly had provided permits under the guise of synagogues and athletic clubs to those dealers willing to pay.[367] Irving Friedman, a Jewish freelance wine agent, was a graft collector between the Prohibition officials and the wine dealers. He later testified that the officers charged $300 to $400 in May 1924 for every two thousand gallons of wine.[368] In the trial of state senator Lowell B. Mason and Major Percy Owen in 1927, Stone served as the chief witness for the government. He testified that, "during the summer of 1924, he collected between $32,000 and 34,000 from Jewish wine dealers and distributors."[369] Though the court ultimately acquitted both Mason and Owen, Stone's testimony is important because he explicitly mentioned the involvement of Jews. It reaffirmed the central role both Chicago Jews and government officials played in the sacramental wine scandal.

On February 23, 1926, the *Forward* reflected on the crime and its impact on the Chicago Jewish community. The author wrote, "We are not interested so much in the number of Jewish bootleggers as we are in the number of rabbis…who make deals with their permits. This action brings shame not only on the Jews as far as the Gentiles are concerned, but also on the Jews as a nation."[370] As always, there was a preoccupation with how the revelations would affect the gentile population's perception of Jews. However, this scandal seemed even more devastating to the Jewish community because some rabbis—the religious leaders and scholars of Jewish law—were also culpable. Furthermore, the phrase "Jews as a nation" has a strong Zionist connotation, implying that the crime had the potential to disgrace the entire transnational Jewish population. To curtail this trouble, the *Forward's* columnist proposed, "[respectable rabbis] should come out openly and condemn their colleagues in the severest manner. Such a step will bring them honor and respect from all the people."[371]

Though there is little evidence suggesting rabbis ousted their colleagues, the bootlegging of sacramental wine did begin to wane, even by the time of the *Forward's* reflection. The change occurred after government officials met with both rabbis and ministers to discuss the future of the wine permit.[372] On December 1, 1925, commissioner of internal revenue David Blair and assistant secretary of the treasury Lincoln Andrews announced the revocation of all existing sacramental wine permits by the year's end and the implementation of new, stringent regulations in 1926.[373] The rules included reducing the maximum allowance of wine for a single family to five gallons a year, in addition to limiting rabbis and ministers to the withdrawal of three months' or less supply at a time.[374] The March 1926 passing of the Cramton Bill also served to decrease the bootlegging of wine by requiring all employees of the Prohibition unit to take competitive exams to ensure morality and placement.[375]

The legislative reform helped to subdue the sacramental wine abuse in the second half of the 1920s. However, its legacy was still felt throughout the Chicago Jewish community. In 1927, for example, Orthodox Jewry in Chicago planned for the development of a *kehillah*—a central communal body, prevalent in Eastern Europe, which acted to strengthen and represent the neighborhood.[376] An article in the *Chicago Jewish Chronicle* argued that a greater budget was necessary for the *kehillah* to address important community activities, like the supervision of wine permits and other Orthodox needs.[377] "The wine scandals will be green in the memory of Chicago Jewry for many years to come. We are certain that if the scandals crop up again…that no power on earth will be able to prevent a scandal that the community will

In a warehouse, a group of men dump wine from barrels into a hole in the ground during Prohibition, Chicago, 1921. *Chicago History Museum, DN-0072930, Chicago Daily News, Inc.*

Captain Joseph Goldberg searches a pantry during a raid of a beer flat in the 4000 block of North Tripp Avenue, Chicago, 1921. *Chicago History Museum, ICHi-03611.*

never be able to live down. It is manifestly a duty of the *kehillah* to take the proper steps to prevent such a scandal."[378]

Jews on the city's West Side, steeped in the ways of Eastern Europe, realized the weight the Prohibition era had placed uniquely on their community. Yet

An advertisement for Edwards Auto Glass in celebration of the end of Prohibition, Chicago, circa 1932. *Chicago History Museum, ICHi-68146.*

they had endured the shame and grew stronger in its aftermath—manifest in the *kehillah*, which came to fruition in 1929.[379] Other traditional functions of the *kehillah* included the collection of local taxes, regulation of business and trade comportment and the supervision of craft guilds and their complex rules.[380] Additionally, the political institution sought to control kosher practices, fundamental to the Jewish Orthodoxy. The organization came, however, after another crime—labor racketeering—had grabbed hold of the community's food trades and economy.

II

The Jewish labor movement, composed largely of Eastern European immigrants, began in 1886 with the infamous Haymarket Riot. Some four hundred immigrant cloak makers left the ghetto and took to the streets to express dissatisfaction with the unbearable working and living conditions they endured. Four years later, the Chicago Cloak Makers Union became the city's first chartered Jewish union.[381] By and large, the garment business became a "Jewish" industry in the late nineteenth and early twentieth centuries, with many of the shops closed on the weekly Sabbath and on the High Holidays.[382] Yet besides activity in the garment industry—the center of a strong, progressive labor movement—the Eastern European Jews were slow in developing their own trade associations. "The Jewish labor movement of Chicago," the *Daily Jewish Courier* bemoaned in 1914, "is a movement sans soul, sans life and sans will-power, the most insignificant one in comparison with the large, general labor movement of Chicago."[383]

As a mass market continued to burgeon in Chicago, however, local craftsmen on the West Side increasingly organized against large corporations to remain relevant in the city's economy and to guard against exploitation from bosses.[384] In 1916, for example, the Jewish butchers organized a union for the first time and met at 3053 West Twelfth Street near Douglas Park to discuss wages and hours in a trade where "most of them simply go hungry."[385] The Jewish Baker's Union Local 237 also organized, as did leagues of Jewish carpenters, cigar makers, fish handlers and *shochtem*—ritual slaughterers.[386] According to Irving Cutler, Jews formed these local unions because the tradesmen "felt more accepted and secure among their kinsmen."[387] In doing so, they built a strong local economy on the West Side and kept corporate employers out. Workers and consumers alike chose to shop in the unionized, local stores where they found familiar goods and faces of the neighborhood.[388] The unions regulated the location of stores, hours of operation and prices and types of products available.[389] In time, certain craftsmen and bosses began to enforce these rules for their own benefit, employing violence and intimidation to maintain order in new, fly-by-night labor associations.[390] It is worth noting that other Jewish gangsters in Chicago, like Simon Gorman and Hirschie Miller, were notable racketeers in various businesses, and as Prohibition came to a close, the Capone gang became highly invested in labor racketeering. Yet it was the existence of labor grafting in the Jewish food trades that affected the West Side community most directly.[391] Indeed, as historian Steven Fraser notes, "What was distinctive about Jewish criminals was their connection, as parasitic racketeers, to the petty business worlds of their ethnic brethren."[392]

The *World*, a Socialist Yiddish daily newspaper, exposed the workings of one such racketeering outfit in its October 19, 1917 article "Jewish Quarter Terrorized by Baker Bosses Association."[393] This group of local bakery owners, under the name "Jewish Master Bakers Association," conspired to "extort more money from the poor working families" by raising the price of bread.[394] With the help of hired gangsters, the group terrorized all bakery bosses who refused to become members of the trust or adhere to price increases by "beating, massacreing [*sic*], setting fire [to bakeries] and saturating bread with kerosene."[395] The *World* recounted the misfortunes of one victim, owner Sam Kazlosky, who left the gang after opposing a new price increase. While Kazlosky was away from his bakery on July 1, gangsters doused his dough with kerosene, and soon after, policemen arrived, ordering the closing of the bakery on account of "unsanitary conditions." This indicated a certain degree of collusion between labor racketeers and policemen, yet Kazlosky's bakery did not close.[396]

Instead, the acts of intimidation continued into the fall. One day, a group of gangsters beat up Kazlosky while he was delivering bread to a nearby grocer, and in September, while the Kazloskys were in synagogue for Yom Kippur, affiliates of the Master Bakers burned down his store.[397] Since Yom Kippur is the holiest day of the year for Jews and one of atonement, it is no surprise the *World* utilized Kazlosky's story to underscore the ruthlessness and sacrilegious nature of the Master Bakers, who terrorized other Jews for economic gain. The newspaper also published the names and addresses of the association's leaders, many of whom lived in the ghetto, to fully expose them to the Jewish community and to warn readers against buying from those bakers' shops.

In light of the *World's* revealing column, there was a public outcry from the Jewish community. It is important to remember that the price fixing did not only affect terrorized owners but also the stores' patrons. In response, the Master Bakers reduced the price of two-and-a-half pound loaves of bread in the Lawndale district—an area of second settlement for Jews—from twenty cents to sixteen cents.[398] However, the association was far from dissolution, and the *Chicago Tribune* soon took notice of the West Side racketeering. On November 16, 1918, the newspaper reported on "one of the loudest and most powerful bombs set off in factional strife" at L. Becker's bakery, just west of Douglas Park. Becker blamed this attack and others on the Hebrew Master Bakers Association because he sold bread for less than the prices set by the gang trust.[399] The following year, small groups of Jewish housewives rioted on West Twelfth Street near Homan Avenue to express their dissatisfaction with the latest proposed price increase by the Master Bakers. Abraham Liebling, publisher of the *Daily Jewish Press*, threatened to turn the names of fourteen Master Bakers over to state's attorney Maclay Hoyne on charges of conspiracy.[400] These two actions, though marginal in success, demonstrate the economic fragility of the Eastern European Jews and just how deeply the increases in bread prices, and thus the racketeering, affected the Jewish community.

The price fixing and racketeering in the Jewish bakers' trade continued to plague the community throughout the 1920s. In the summer of 1927, a crowd of five thousand Jewish residents gathered in the vicinity of Kedzie Avenue, between Thirteenth and Sixteenth Streets, to protest yet another increase in the price of bread. Some stole loaves from stores while others threatened to boycott the bakeries. In response, fifty policemen of the Fillmore Street station arrived to protect the Jewish bakeries from the disorder.[401] As the year progressed, special assistant state's attorney Walter Walker investigated the Jewish Master Bakers Association and learned more about the racketeers. Walker found that the association's officers collected an initiation fee of $200 and weekly dues of $13 from member bakery owners, but he could not identify any real advantages derived from paying these exorbitant fees to the association, save the avoidance of "troubles."[402]

The Master Bakers had become a highly organized racketeering group that increasingly terrorized not only the recalcitrant bakery owners but also the stores served. By raising the price of a staple food like bread, the Master Bakers undermined a relatively poor community. Evidently, the association was not the only one of its kind. An article by Thomas Wren that hit the stands on November 27, 1917, proclaimed, "The 75,000 Jewish residents of the West Side are the hardest hit by the machinations of Chicago racketeers. Prices of virtually all their food stuffs are fixed by agreement between a few gangster racketeers and a few sophisticated merchant members of the fly-by-night associations."[403] According to the report, Maxie Eisen was the head of the Hebrew Master Bakers, the Wholesale and Retail Fish Dealers' association and the Hebrew Master Butchers and brought in an annual income of $50,000 to $60,000 from these fraudulent business dealings.[404]

Racketeering in the animal food trades—more specifically, in the Hebrew Butchers' and Schechters' Associations—was especially troublesome to the Orthodox community because Jewish dietary laws, known collectively as *kashrut*, tethered the residents to these stores and their prices. Meaning "fit" or "proper," *kashrut* embodies the Jewish laws and customs derived from Bible passages that dictate which types of food are allowed for consumption and their proper preparation.[405] Jews may consume animals deemed *tahor*, or clean, if prepared properly, whereas they must never eat those considered *tame*, or unclean. *Kashrut* also prescribes that a trained slaughterer—the *schochet*—must abide by a number of strict regulations, such as the use of a sharp knife without any chips or imperfections. The *schochet* "must cut both the esophagus and trachea with continuous strokes," and stricter standards of kashrut require an examination for diseases or defects of the animal's vital organs.[406] A food that satisfies the Jewish laws is kosher. Historian Andrew Cohen notes that Jews' consumption of kosher meat in Chicago "demonstrated not only obedience to God's law, but also a dedication to Old World culture and a reluctance to assimilate."[407] Whether or not Chicago Jewry consciously resisted assimilation, the animal food industry was particularly significant to the Jewish community for religious, cultural and economic reasons. Cohen's analysis further reinforces the Jews' reliance on local kosher butcheries during the 1920s and 1930s—an industry that Jewish racketeers like Maxie Eisen penetrated.

In 1925, the state's attorney set out to smash the trust of racketeers in order to free the "honest small dealer from the yoke of oppression by tribute levying thugs kicked out of union labor."[408] Maxie Eisen, cited as the organizer of the Hebrew Master Butchers' Association, was one of the gangsters indicted in this special grand jury investigation for allegedly throwing a stink bomb into Isaac Herbert's meat market. However, when the court called his case nine months later, the prosecuting witness had passed away.[409] His acts of intimidation against Jewish butcher and meat stores, chronicled in John Landesco's *Organized Crime in Chicago*, continued to surface throughout the 1920s with little hindrance from law enforcement.[410]

Yet in October 1931, Chicago's newfound *kehillah*, the ruling body of prominent Orthodox rabbis and laymen, took a stand against Maxie Eisen's recent appointment as business agent of the Hebrew Butchers' union. The *kehillah* threatened to ban the consumption of all meat by Orthodox Jewry unless the union ousted Eisen, who promised greater profits for the struggling butchers. The *kehillah* observed that kosher meat prices had increased 50 percent or more since the Hebrew Butchers' Association employed Eisen. In a public statement, the religious order expressed, "They [the union] had no right to engage a public enemy and racketeer to handle their business. Such a procedure is a disgrace to the community, contrary to Jewish law and a violation of traditions."[411] It is interesting that the *kehillah* faulted the union more than Eisen for his labor racketeering. This intimated that they held the butchers (men from the community) to a higher standard than Eisen (a public enemy and outcast to Chicago Jewry). It is also significant that the *kehillah* underscored the shame the union brought to the neighborhood and to Judaism. This served as both a condemnation of labor racketeering and a demonstration to Chicago gentiles that such activity was intolerable.

On October 11, the *kehillah* called a meeting with twenty-five members of the union as an ultimatum before the meat ban. The butchers argued that the religious body had no right to dictate who could or could not be an officer of the union, and the *Chicago Tribune* described the conference as a "stormy session."[412] Their resistance spoke to the low economic standing of the Jewish butchers and the need to earn higher wages. Surely the butchers did not condone Eisen's violent tactics, especially since it was they themselves who often suffered the consequences. Yet it was through these methods and the enforcement of price increases that greater profits were secured for the butchers. Labor racketeering in the Jewish community, then, was oftentimes a story of economic mobility for wage earners and employers who did not otherwise have access to such gains. Nonetheless, the meeting between members of the *kehillah* and the union ended in Eisen's resignation, which evaded a community ban of kosher meat. Despite resolving to organize the butchers on a non-racketeering basis, in 1932 the detective bureau formally charged Abraham Yampolsky, the new president of the Hebrew Butchers' Association, and member Joseph Arshinov in the bombing of two nonassociation meat markets.[413]

The Chicago rabbinate faced a similar situation with the Schechters' (Hebrew chicken butchers) Union in 1930. The confrontation revealed more about the relationship between Judaism and racketeering, the solidarity of American Jewry and the persistence of labor corruption in the city. There had been widespread labor grafting and great internal strife between *shochtem*, the authorized slaughterers of poultry under *kashrut*, ever since Joseph Etkin had become the union's controversial business agent. In 1929, the court indicted Etkin on charges of conspiracy in the fire of Anna Bergowitz's chicken-killing plant.[414] Rabbis initially remained quiet and distant from the affair, with one telling the *Tribune*, "To mention my name with the Etkin charges would mean my death."[415] This was perhaps because outspoken rabbis received threats from Etkin and his associates, who had no respect for the religious leaders. Nonetheless, with the establishment of the *kehillah* in 1929, the Chicago rabbinate took a united stand against the poultry tradesmen in December 1930.

The governing body of the Orthodox Jews declared a ban on poultry, effective Monday, December 29, 1930, and boldly dictated that no fowl found in Orthodox Jewish markets would be kosher after that date until the ban's end.[416] The Talmud, the rabbis contended, required "clean and pious men for holy killings," and the terrorism, racketeering and slugging employed by certain *shochtem* violated this demand.[417] Moreover, the *kehillah* charged that many *shochtem* ignored the monthly examinations by Jewish laws before the religious board, such as the inspection of knives to ensure there were no imperfections on the blades.[418] The reasons for accusation were serious and pitted racketeering directly against the statutes of Judaism.

Following a meeting with three hundred representatives

CHICKEN KILLERS STRIKE IN REPLY TO BAN OF RABBIS

350,000 Jews Have No Poultry.

(Picture on back page.)

The dispute between the council of rabbis of the Chicago rabbinate and the officers of the Shochtim, authorized organization of kosher poultry killers, over charges of racketeering and terrorism against some of the Shochtim leaders, tied up the kosher poultry business yesterday.

The rabbinate had declared a ban on kosher poultry, effective yesterday, until the Shochtim had been purged of its evil elements. In retaliation, the Shochtim leaders declared the poultry killers were on strike.

The rabbinate council announced it would not lift its ban until the Shochtim is once again under the rule of the council, as Mosaic law prescribes. The union retorted that the strike will not be lifted until the Shochtim is completely divorced from rabbinical control.

This page and next: A newspaper headline during the ban on chicken, 1930. *From the* Chicago Tribune, *December 30, 1930.*

Jews to Obey Edict.

The rabbis said the strike was an example of "sour grapes," pointing out that, strike or no strike, the Shochtim could not work without permission of the council. They also say that the 350,000 Orthodox Jews of the city will refuse to buy poultry until the Shochtim is purified.

The ban on poultry permits the selling only of poultry killed before noon yesterday. As soon as that supply is exhausted, the orthodox Chicago Jews will be without kosher poultry for the first time in the history of the city.

The rabbinical decree makes the lifting of the ban dependent on the suspension of all six officers of the Shochtim and a return to the control of the council. The action follows an alleged reign of terror in which slugging, ruining of poultry, and bombing of butcher shops, said to have been instigated by union officers, kept the six officers in power against the will of the members.

Oppression Is Charged.

Many shochtim have appealed to members of the rabbinical council for protection, according to the rabbis, asserting that their wages are being confiscated as union dues and that they must pay for choice jobs. Some shochtim, through favoritism, earn from $100 to $250 a week, while others are fortunate to earn $25, after paying $300 to enter the union, it is charged. All day yesterday members of the union telephoned the rabbinical council to approve the action, according to the rabbis, but the union on Sunday voted confidence in its officers and unanimously ordered a strike.

of fifty synagogues in Chicago, the council of rabbis released four conditions the *shochtem* had to agree upon before they lifted the ban. The ritual slaughterers had to "abide by the dictates of the council of rabbis" and allow this religious authority to settle "all differences between individual kosher shop owners and shochets."[419] Additionally, "all executives and officials of the Shochtim" had to resign, and "no layman" could be "business manager of the Shochtim"; instead, a schochet had to fill this position.[420] In turn, these "peace offerings" centered on the deference of the *shochtem* to the rule of the Chicago rabbinate—a prescription in Mosaic law that had been disregarded— and demonstrated the unity of the prominent Orthodox Jewish leaders.[421] In response, the *shochtem* leaders proclaimed that the poultry killers were now on strike, but the rabbis called this action "sour grapes." After all, strike or no strike, the Shochtim could not work without permission from the Chicago rabbinate.[422]

The *kehillah* received support both locally and nationally. On December 30, the *Chicago Tribune* published a powerful photograph that portrayed the community's response to the ban. The picture shows Ben Rubin, a poultry dealer at 913 Maxwell

Street, offering to sell Mrs. E. Wexler a goose despite the rabbis' wishes. Mrs. Wexler proudly declined the goose, raising both hands in front of the peddler to express her disinterest.[423] It was no doubt a staged photograph, as the dealer, Mrs. Wexler and a female bystander are all smiling. Nonetheless, it is significant because the newspaper chose that picture to represent the sentiment of the Jewish community. Furthermore, the *Chicago Tribune* reported that Orthodox Jews throughout North America pledged their support in the fight to drive racketeering from the Shochtim. A telegram from the rabbinate of America in New York, who suffered from similar labor exploitation, commended the actions of the Chicago council members.[424] The wide support spoke to the great publicity the war on racketeering garnered in the newspapers, as well as the national cohesion of Orthodox Jewish leaders.

On January 6, 1931, eight days after the initial poultry prohibition, members of the *kehillah* and the newly elected officers of the shochtem met to announce the lifting of the ban.[425] All four conditions of the rabbis were met, and the shochtem forced their former officers out of the union. Rabbi Menahem Sachs, president of the *kehillah*, praised all Jews who observed the ban and applauded members of the Kosher Butchers' Association, who collectively lost nearly $100,000 in poultry sales and wages.[426] The rabbis' war on racketeering in the poultry trade demonstrated the character and resolve of the Chicago Orthodox rabbis, loyal members of the Schechters' Union and the Jewish community to bring dignity back to the industry.

The 1920s and early 1930s brought the scandal in sacramental wine and labor racketeering to the forefront of affairs in the Chicago Jewish community. The bootlegging in wine spotlighted the pronounced social, economic and religious differences between the Reform and Orthodox Jews. It reinforced the fact that Reform Jews were more affluent than their Orthodox counterparts, and perhaps in resentment, the Orthodox maintained that they were the Judaic authority on religious questions, such as the necessity of sacramental wine. Labor racketeering illuminated the internal strife among the Orthodox Jewish community and commented on its economic standing and religious values, as well as the authoritative role of the Chicago rabbinate. Indeed, bootlegging and racketeering revealed two conflicting faces of the Orthodox rabbis—one as criminals and the other as reformers—and best relates the increasing directorship and centralization of the religious leaders as the 1920s proceeded. The crimes also conveyed the dispersal of Eastern European Jews in Chicago from the ghetto to areas of second settlement, such as the Lawndale district and Douglas Park.

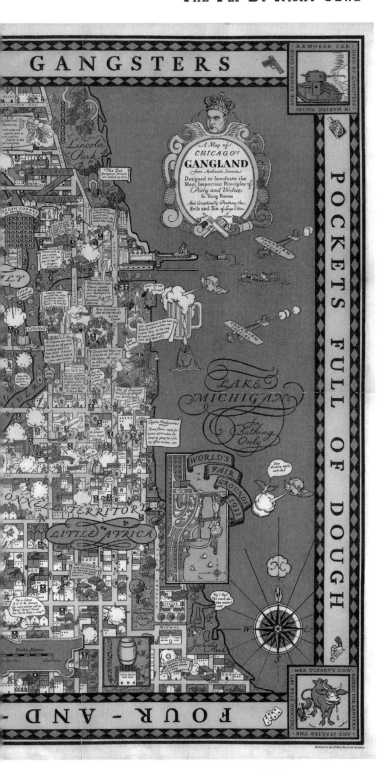

A colorful map of Chicago and its gangland, 1931. *Courtesy of the Newberry Library, Chicago. Call No.: map G 10896 .548.*

The city's Jews, however, were not alone in their struggle to make sense of and combat the two criminal ventures. Jews in New York and other major metropolises also grappled with the wrongdoings.[427] More broadly, then, bootlegging and racketeering reflected the national network of American Jewry that prevailed, the commonality of Jews in crime and the endeavor of all Jewish immigrants to progress in the city's standings while still grasping hold of their own unique identity.

CONCLUSION

The path that leads out of the ghetto is neither straight nor unobstructed. No sooner does the Jew venture forth from the narrow ghetto streets into the broad cosmopolitan life of the outer world than he encounters external obstacles and experiences inner conflicts. [428]
—*Louis Wirth, 1928*

There are a number of elements that go into the shaping of an urban ethnic community, including language, cultural traditions, commerce and institution building. This process was no different for the German and Eastern European Jewish immigrants who arrived in Chicago during the nineteenth and early twentieth centuries. However, today's Chicago Jewry and scholars alike have overlooked—or, in some cases, deliberately forgotten—a factor that was critical to the development of the Jewish community: crime. In the first thirty-five years of the twentieth century, Jewish crime played a prominent role in forming the Chicago Jewish community on the West Side, and it provides a unique lens through which to view the inhabitants' urban experience and maturation.

Looking at crime uncovers a great deal about the situation of the Jews. The limited economic and social mobility afforded in the ghetto motivated people of all ages and occupations to turn to delinquent activities in order to move up in the city's hierarchy. It touched sons and daughters, butchers and bakers, community leaders and rabbis. The vices exposed the corruption of local politicians and policemen and also demonstrated the intricate workings of the Chicago underworld. Furthermore, Jewish crime helped to shape the gentiles' perception of the city's Jews and the prevalence of anti-Semitism. Consequently, the Jewish community, often through the Yiddish press, defended their reputation and distanced themselves from the shame. It forced the ghetto's dwellers to self-consciously look inward to make sense of the criminality that challenged the fundamentals of their social and religious values and revealed the tensions between Reform and Orthodox Jews. Above all, crime in the early twentieth century left a significant imprint on the identity of Chicago Jewry that remained long after its population had dispersed north, south and west of the ghetto.

By the middle of the 1920s, the Maxwell Street ghetto had already begun to decline as Jews migrated out of their familiar West Side community to surrounding neighborhoods.[429] Signs of the "vanishing ghetto," a phrase coined by sociologist Louis Wirth, manifested itself in several forms. Statistics taken from the 1914 and 1923 school years show that the number of Jewish children enrolled in Maxwell Street–area public schools diminished markedly. At Goodrich school, for example, the percentage of Jewish students decreased by 63 percent—from 736 pupils in 1914 to just 23 by 1923.[430] Others, like Medill Grade School, closed altogether. Institutions began to move with the Jewish population, too. The change in synagogue distribution was remarkable, with the greatest concentration of congregations shifting west of the ghetto.[431] In 1926, the Jewish People's Institute—formerly known as the Chicago Hebrew Institute—also moved west to Lawndale after twenty-two years of service in the Maxwell Street district. This community center, which held concerts, dances, sporting events and a variety of classes, had offered more for the residents than most could have afforded elsewhere.[432]

The most telling signal of the ghetto's closing, however, was the decline in Yiddish newspapers. The smaller papers went first. The *Daily Jewish Call*—established in 1905—ceased publication in 1924. The weekly *Jewish Times* followed suit in 1929. Similarly, the *Daily Jewish Press*, located at 1107 South Halsted Street in the heart of the ghetto, stopped in 1934 after thirty-three years of print.[433] Even the *Daily Jewish Courier*, the voice of Orthodox Jewry that was instrumental in shaping the community's views toward crime and other affairs, succumbed to the changing times. Its readership continued to decline throughout the 1930s, and after over fifty years of daily newspapers, the organ of the Maxwell Street ghetto closed in 1944.[434]

As the population moved into areas of second and third settlement, those neighborhoods, not surprisingly, became predominantly Jewish. However, their makeup was not the same. In 1928, Louis Wirth noted, "Lawndale is an area of transition in which the character of the ghetto is being remolded under the influences of wider contacts and a larger world."[435] The Orthodox Jews were no longer immersed in a community characterized by their Old World culture, and younger generations of Jews spoke English over Yiddish.[436] Moreover, the "vanishing ghetto" afforded its former population a relative increase in economic mobility, and Orthodox Jews began to rise in society as "Americans."

Indeed, the Jews moved with purpose out of the Maxwell Street ghetto. There was a fit between the geographic mobility on the one hand and the social and economic mobility on the other. This upward advancement, coupled with an increase in respectability and a relative decrease in American anti-Semitism, corresponded to a decline of Jewish crime and gangsters in the city and its significance to Chicago Jewry. The closing of the ghetto was, in many ways, the end to the "Jewish gangster." Newspapers increasingly omitted the religious marker. Accordingly, Jewish criminals became simply "gangsters." The population dispersal indicated that the interaction between the gentile population, the Jewish community and the Jewish panderer, gambler or racketeer would no longer be so pronounced. The gangsters' activities could not hold the same significance or affect Chicago Jewry as they once did. For example, the *Chicago Tribune* could not blame Jews for crimes using the sweeping terms of old, such as the "ghetto" or "Russian Jews," because they simply did not apply. In turn, the gangsters did not affront the reputation of a single Jewish community, and their impact diminished.

Wirth postulated that Chicago Jewry and its institutions were "a product of the ghetto."[437] I contend that crime, too, was a result of the ghetto. Even after its decline, though, the ghetto's legacy on Jewish vice lived on. Jewish involvement in organized crime groups like the Chicago Outfit was emblematic of the ghetto's longer-lasting repercussions. The run-down streets and tenements of the Maxwell Street community, as well as the limited social and economic opportunities it offered, drove many criminals even deeper into the city's underworld and away from the neighborhood altogether. Unlike Julius and Louis Frank or Alderman Manny Abrahams, success in crime moved these gangsters well outside of the ghetto, residing, instead, nearer to the Loop. They disassociated themselves from their childhoods in the West Side community and had little to do with Jewish affairs.

Yet these gangsters were exceptions to the rule. One such anomaly was Jack "Greasy Thumb" Guzik, who started in the prostitution business and rose to business manager and chief lieutenant to Al Capone. George Bliss, a Pulitzer Prize–winning journalist for the *Chicago Tribune*, posthumously observed in 1956 that Guzik was born in the West Side ghetto in 1887.[438] Newspaper articles rarely made mention of his religious affiliation, though some of the descriptions were quite suggestive of the Jewish stereotype. "Small of stature, baggy eyed, and flabby," a *Chicago Tribune* columnist noted, "Guzik did not fit any popular conception of a gang boss. He resembled, instead, a mild mannered retired grocer or clerk."[439]

Guzik's rise to a sustained, high position in Al Capone's gang occurred sometime during the 1920s. By 1930, he was number ten on the original list of twenty-eight public enemies assembled by the Chicago Crime Commission. The same year, the federal courts tried and convicted both Capone and Guzik for tax fraud, sentencing them, respectively, to eleven and five years in prison.[440]

After three years and eight months, the courts released Jack Guzik, though this did not mean the end of his legal troubles. On June 7, 1939, for example, a notice from the First Collection District, State of Illinois, to Mr. John Guzik of 7240 Luella Avenue read, "You are hereby notified that there

Jake Guzik (front, second from right) and brother Sam (front left) in a Chicago courthouse, 1930. *Chicago History Museum, DN-0093611, Chicago Daily News, Inc.*

Portrait of Jake Guzik, Chicago, circa 1930. *Chicago History Museum, DN-D-8761, Chicago Daily News, Inc.*

is now due, owing and unpaid from John (Jack) Guzik to the United States of America the sum of Tax $503,190.10; Interest: $125, 597.61."[441]

As Capone's influence waned during his prison sentence in Alcatraz and afterward, Guzik's flourished. He masterminded the Syndicate's takeover and consolidation of Chicago gambling throughout the late 1930s and 1940s.[442] In 1941, a *Chicago Tribune* headline read, "Jack Guzik Now Is No. 1 Man of Gang Overlords," placing him in front of gangsters Frank Nitti, Murray Humphreys and Edward Vogel.[443] He continued to remain the subject of fascination in newspaper stories up until his death in the mid-1950s. In 1954, Ben Lindheimer, the track-managing director of Arlington Park racetrack, barred Guzik from entry after believing the longtime gangster was moving in on the "race business."[444] In response, Guzik, then sixty-seven, filed a lawsuit against Lindheimer, maintaining, "Those racing people are all a lot of phonies."[445] Guzik died of a heart attack two years later, before the conclusion of his lawsuit. Nearly four hundred mourners paid their final respects, including several First Ward politicians, Chicago Outfit boss Tony Accardo and Matt Capone (the youngest brother of "Scarface" who had played ball with my great-uncle in Columbus Park during the 1920s).[446]

The life of Jack Guzik—a Jew from the West Side—reaffirmed the reciprocal relationship between crime and the Maxwell Street ghetto that was there all along. During the early twentieth century, crime indelibly shaped and left a mark on the Chicago Jewish community. Yet it was the conditions of the ghetto that produced and shaped its gangsters. With the ghetto all but gone by the mid-1930s and into the 1940s, the relative significance of Jewish crime on the community also diminished, and many families chose to leave behind the memories of this formative influence.

NOTES

Introduction

1. Marshall Peiros, interview by author, Deerfield, IL, March 1, 2011.
2. See Landesco, *Organized Crime in Chicago*; Asbury, *Gem of the Prairie*; Asbury, *Great Illusion*; Asbury, *Sucker's Progress*.
3. Joselit, *Our Gang*, 13. See also Goren, *New York Jews*; Cohen, *Tough Jews*.
4. Haller, "Ethnic Crime," 564. See also O'Kane, *Crooked Ladder*.
5. Cutler, *Jews of Chicago*, 64.
6. Since I cannot read Yiddish, I worked extensively with newspaper articles published and translated in the Chicago Foreign Language Press Survey (CFLPS). This digitized collection provided me with access to select articles from key periodicals of the Jewish community, such as the *Daily Jewish Courier* and the *Forward*. It is worth remembering, however, that English translations can be problematic, as they might result in mistranslations that affect the original meaning of the articles. Additionally, members of the Chicago Jewish community translated the articles in the CFLPS well after the original date of publication. In turn, the translations might reflect their own biases that present their community in the best of light. While I was always cognizant of these precautions, the opportunity to analyze the voices of the Jewish newspapers, a largely untapped resource in the works of other scholars, outweighs the challenges it affords.

CHAPTER I

7. *Chicago Daily Tribune*, "Our Russian Exiles," July 19, 1891, http://www. proquest.com (accessed November 20, 2011).

8. Observed by Colbee C. Benton, a young merchant from New Hampshire, in his diary while visiting Chicago in 1833. See Benton, *Prairie State*, 115.

9. Butler, *As Others See Chicago*, 45.

10. Meites, *History of the Jews*, 35–36.

11. Ibid., 37.

12. Ibid., 39.

13. Wirth, *Ghetto*, 153–54.

14. Meites, *History of the Jews*, 41–42.

15. I drove by the cemetery this past summer. See Cutler, *Jews of Chicago*, 10.

16. Ibid., 11.

17. Wirth, *Ghetto*, 158.

18. Levine, *Spirit of 1848*, 15.

19. Ibid., 20.

20. Ibid., 35.

21. Wirth, *Ghetto*, 158.

22. Ibid., 160.

23. Cutler, *Jews of Chicago*, 15.

24. Levine, *Spirit of 1848*, 48.

25. Cutler, *Jews of Chicago*, 16.

26. Wirth, *Ghetto*, 161.

27. Ibid., 164.

28. Cutler, *Jews of Chicago*, 24.

29. Ibid., 28.

30. *Chicago Daily Tribune*, "Cheer Up," October 11, 1871, http://www. proquest.com (accessed November 1, 2011).

31. Wirth, *Ghetto*, 171–72.

32. *Chicago Daily Tribune*, "The Fires," July 16, 1874, http://www.proquest. com (accessed November 1, 2011).

33. Wirth., *Ghetto*, 172.

34. Ibid., 173. See also Meites, *History of the Jews*, 133.

35. Wirth, *Ghetto*, 173.

36. Cutler, *Jews of Chicago*, 52.

37. Wirth, *Ghetto*, 182.

38. Cutler, *Jews of Chicago*, 56.

39. Wirth, *Ghetto*, 180.

40. Ibid., 181.

41. Ibid., 182. For more on the German Jewry's motivations to come to America, including firsthand testimony, see Levine, *Spirit of 1848*, 54.

42. Wirth, *Ghetto*, 1. Wirth defines the concept of "the ghetto" as the Jewish quarter of a city. See also Abbott, *Tenements of Chicago*, 86.

43. Cutler, *Jews of Chicago*, 42.

44. Ibid., 44.

45. Abbott, *Tenements of Chicago*, 88.

46. Wirth, *Ghetto*, 184.

47. Ibid.

48. Abbott, *Tenements of Chicago*, 86.

49. Ibid., 260.

50. *Chicago Daily Tribune*, "Our Russian Exiles."

51. Cutler, *Jews of Chicago*, 60.

52. *Chicago Daily Tribune* "Our Russian Exiles."

53. Ibid.

54. Bregstone, *Chicago and Its Jews*, 69.

55. Ibid.

56. Committee on Crime of the City of Chicago, March 22, 1915, "A Study of Cook County Boys Now in the St. Charles Reformatory," Charles E. Merriam Papers, 132.

57. Ibid., 133.

58. Korey, "History of Jewish Education," 3.

59. Ibid., 4.

60. See Korey, "History of Jewish Education."

61. Ibid.

62. Hansen, "Problem of Third Generation Immigrant," 191.

63. Ibid., 192–93.

64. Ibid., 193.

65. O'Kane, *Crooked Ladder*, 28.

66. Haller, "Ethnic Crime," 558.

67. Ibid., 558–59.

68. Diamond, *Mean Streets*, 5.

69. Thrasher, *The Gang*, 8.

70. Ibid., 9–12.

CHAPTER 2

71. Bisno, *Union Pioneer*, 56.

72. *Chicago Daily Tribune*, "Tenement Conditions in Chicago Report of Investigation by the City Homes Association," June 2, 1901, http://www.proquest.com (accessed November 23, 2011).

73. Polacheck, *I Came a Stranger*, 29–30.

74. For a more complete description of the Maxwell Street market, see Cutler, *Jews of Chicago*, 66.

75. *Chicago Daily Tribune*, "Table of Contents 1—No Title." March 25, 1901, http://www.proquest.com (accessed November 25, 2011).

76. *Chicago Daily Tribune*, "Woes of the Peddlers: Jewish Merchants Hold an Indignation Meeting," March 25, 1901, http://www.proquest.com (accessed November 20, 2011). See also *Illinois Staats-Leitung*, "Jewish Peddlers." According to *Oxford English Dictionary* Online, "sheeney" (also spelled sheeny and sheenie) is a disparaging and offensive slang word for "Jew."

77. *Chicago Daily Tribune*, "Arrest Boy Jew Baiters," February 10, 1906, http://www.proquest.com (accessed November 25, 2011).

78. Ibid.

79. *Chicago Daily Tribune*, "Plan War on Jew Baiters: Ghetto Residents Organize in Self-Defense," November 21, 1906, http://www.proquest.com (accessed November 25, 2011).

80. Frederick W. Wile. "America Leads in Bias Against Jew," *Chicago Daily Tribune*, September 7, 1908, http://www.proquest.com (accessed November 20, 2011).

81. Bisno, *Union Pioneer*, 55. For a contrasting account, see Polacheck, *I Came a Stranger*, 51. One of Hilda's Irish playmates introduced her to the Hull House so the two ethnic groups did befriend one another on occasion.

82. *Daily Jewish Courier*, "Valley Gang Attacks Jew," November 24, 1913. For more on the Valley Gang, see Thrasher, *The Gang*, 382, 424, 431, 433.

83. *Daily Jewish Courier*, "It Must Not Be Hushed Up," August 2, 1916.

84. Thrasher, *The Gang*, 195.

85. Frazier Hunt, "Russ Jews Fear Monsterpogrom in a New Revolt," *Chicago Daily Tribune*, May 25, 1919, http://www.proquest.com (accessed November 23, 2011).

86. *Chicago Daily Tribune*, "Report 54 Jews Pogrom Victims in Two Months," May 27, 1919, http://www.proquest.com (accessed November 20, 2011).

87. *Daily Jewish Courier*, "Chicago Poles Could Not Stage a Pogrom Yesterday," June 9, 1919.

88. Ibid.

89. For another Polish pogrom against a Chicago Jew, see J. Leobner, "On the Community Stage," *Sunday Jewish Courier*, July 27, 1919.

90. J. Leobner, "The Bums in Stanford Park," *Sunday Jewish Courier*, January 25, 1924.

91. Thrasher, *The Gang*, 191.

92. Ibid., 74.

93. *Chicago Daily Tribune*, "Site For West Side Park Purchased for $200,000," July 19, 1908, http://www.proquest.com (accessed November 20, 2011).

94. Thrasher, *The Gang*, 137.

95. Ibid., 74.

96. *Chicago Daily Tribune*, "Breaking Up Boys' Gangs," March 13, 1906, http://www.proquest.com (accessed November 20, 2011). For more on the longstanding schoolboy feud at Walsh School, see Asbury, *Gem of the Prairie*, 212.

97. *Chicago Daily Tribune*, "School Race War Costs Boy's Life," March 11, 1906, http://www.proquest.com (accessed November 20, 2011).

98. *Chicago Daily Tribune*, "Breaking Up Boys' Gangs."

99. E.M. Wolfson, "The Young Gangster in Chicago," *Daily Jewish Courier*, November 6, 1913.

100. Thrasher, *The Gang*, 191–92.

101. Ibid., 220. See also, Cutler, *Jews of Chicago*, 125.

102. Thrasher, *The Gang*, 214.

103. Ibid., 12.

104. Ibid.

105. Ibid., 174.

106. Landesco, *Organized Crime in Chicago*, 245.

107. *Daily Jewish Courier*, "Chief Gleason Praises Detective Weisbaum," May 18, 1914. However, an investigator's report from November 1914 reveals the names of several Jewish pickpockets and thieves who "have been passed by second-class detective sergeants Wisebaum [*sic*]...of Maxwell Street Station regularly for protection." See "Report of No. 100," November 10, 1914, Charles E. Merriam Papers. For more on the collusion between Chicago police and pickpockets in 1914, see "Letter to Merriam Complaining About Pickpockets in Court," October 15, 1914, Charles E. Merriam Papers.

108. *Chicago Daily Tribune*, "Haunts of Pickpockets and Protection by Police Revealed," October 8, 1914, http://www.proquest.com (accessed November 20, 2011). This article also includes the intricate system of operations employed by pickpocket outfits.

109. *Itschkie*, Yiddish for "Izzie," was the longstanding leader of the Black Handers in the early twentieth century. See Thrasher, *The Gang*, 312.

110. See Asbury, *Gem of the Prairie*, 231–36.

111. Ibid., 310.

112. Ibid., 311.

113. Ibid., 317. The Roamer's Inn is not to be confused with "Roamer Inn," a disorderly house kept by Jewish gangster Harry Guzik and his wife, Alma, during the 1920s. See *Chicago Daily Tribune*, "Roadhouse Raid Nets 14 Women; Crowe in Drive," March 6, 1922, http://www.proquest.com (accessed November 21, 2011).

114. Asbury, *Gem of the Prairie*, 315.

115. Ibid., 316.

116. Wirth, *Ghetto*, 192. See also, Cutler, *Jews of Chicago*, 119.

117. *Daily Jewish Courier*. "Thousands of Jews Participate in Double Celebration," July 2, 1917.

118. *Chicago Hebrew Institute Observer*, December 1918–January 1919.

119. Ibid.

120. Thrasher, *The Gang*, 196.

121. Ibid., 197.

122. Though explained with greater detail in chapter one, see Cutler, *Jews of Chicago*, 94, and Wirth, *Ghetto*, 183, for more on the early relationship between German and Eastern European Jews.

123. *Jewish Daily Courier*, "Revolver Heroes Among Jews," July 15, 1912.

124. *Daily Jewish Forward*, "Purify the West Side," July 14, 1914. See also Dr. S.M. Melamed, "Good Morning!" *Daily Jewish Courier*, July 2, 1917.

125. *Chicago Jewish Chronicle*, week of June 6, 1924.

126. For an example of the heat and its effect on the ghetto's inhabitants, see *Chicago Daily Tribune*, "Hot Wave Leads Fourth," July 4, 1900, http://www.proquest.com (accessed December, 26, 2011).

127. Wirth, *Ghetto*, 218.

128. Moses Levin, "Living Orphans," *Daily Jewish Courier*, May 20, 1913.

129. Ibid.

130. *Daily Jewish Courier*, "Thou Shalt Not Kill," February 27, 1914.

131. This testimony is strikingly similar to contentions advanced in Hansen, "Problem of Third Generation Immigrant," 191.

132. *Daily Jewish Courier*, "What Must be Done in Order to Prevent Children From Committing Crimes," March 30, 1923.

133. Cutler, *Jews of Chicago*, 85.

134. *Daily Jewish Courier*, "Institute Day," March 10, 1914.

135. J. Leobner, "From the Public Rostrum," *Daily Jewish Courier*, April 13, 1923. The author, James Bernard Leobner, was an active member of the literary group "Yung Chicago" and well respected. See Cutler, *Jews of Chicago*, 139.

136. *Daily Jewish Courier*, "Thousands of Jews Participate in Double Celebration."

CHAPTER 3

137. Flynt, "In the World of Graft," 334.

138. Tebbel, *American Magazine*, 159.

139. Ibid., 158.

140. *Chicago Daily Tribune*, "Writer Dead," November 5, 1933, http://www.proquest.com (accessed January, 18, 2012). Incidentally, Shepherd died less than two months following the printing of "How to Make a Gangster."

141. Flynt, "In the World of Graft," 334.

142. Asbury, *Gem of the Prairie*, 31, 37.

143. Ibid.

144. Ibid., 38. According to *Oxford English Dictionary* Online, tippling houses are places where liquors are sold in small quantities, for in-house consumption, and similar to barrooms.

145. *Chicago Daily Tribune*, "Liquor Traffic of Chicago," January 30, 1854, http://www.proquest.com (accessed January 21, 2012). Not by coincidence, the deteriorating economy of 1857 compounded the spike of crime in Chicago. See Asbury, *Gem of the Prairie*, 49–50.

146. Ibid.

147. Asbury, *Gem of the Prairie*, 204.

148. *Chicago Daily Tribune*, "The Wickedest District in the World," February 6, 1909, http://www.proquest.com (accessed January 21, 2012).

149. Ibid.

150. Asbury, *Gem of the Prairie*, 211.

151. *Chicago Daily Tribune*, "Levee Invading the Ghetto," October 21, 1907, http://www.proquest.com (accessed January 15, 2012).

152. Ibid.

153. *Chicago Daily Tribune*, "Urge Prison for Levee's 'Farmers,'" December 28, 1907, http://www.proquest.com (accessed January 15, 2012).

154. *Chicago Daily Tribune*, "Shuts Bars at Twelve O'Clock," December 30, 1900, http://www.proquest.com (accessed January 15, 2012).

155. *Chicago Daily Tribune*, "Ax Falls on Levee Resorts; Mayor Shuts Three Saloons," May 23, 1903, http://www.proquest.com (accessed January 15, 2012). For more on Harrison's early vows to clean up the levee district, see Asbury, *Gem of the Prairie*, 204–07.

156. *Chicago Daily Tribune*, "Shuts Bars at Twelve O'Clock."

157. Asbury, *Gem of the Prairie*, 207.

158. *Chicago Daily Tribune*, "Chicago Police Found Wanting," March 20, 1904, http://www.proquest.com (accessed January 15, 2012).

159. August 15, 1914, "Relative to Bruders West-end Club," Charles E. Merriam Papers.

160. November 19, 1914, "Report of Investigator Friedner for Thursday, Nov. 19th 1914," Charles E. Merriam Papers.

161. November 27, 1914, "Report of Number 100," Charles E. Merriam Papers.

162. *Chicago Daily Tribune*, "How Gangs of Boy Bandits Terrorize Chicago," January 28, 1906, http://www.proquest.com (accessed January 18, 2012). See also Landesco, *Organized Crime in Chicago*, 284.

163. *Chicago Daily Tribune*, "Chicago's Boy Gangsters Its Greatest Menace," November 2, 1913, http://www.proquest.com (accessed January 18, 2012).

164. Ibid.

165. Landesco, "Crime and the Failure of Institutions," 247.

166. Landesco, *Organized Crime in Chicago*, 284. In this passage, Landesco also cites Thrasher, *The Gang*, and C.R. Shaw's report entitled "The Nature and Extent of Juvenile Delinquency."

167. Committee on Crime of the City of Chicago, March 22, 1915, "A Study of Cook County Boys Now in the St. Charles Reformatory," Charles E. Merriam Papers, 16.

168. *Daily Jewish Forward*, March 23, 1924.

169. *Chicago Daily Tribune*, "Says Playgrounds End 'Boss,'" January 24, 1911, http://www.proquest.com (accessed January 22, 2012). See also Addams, *New Conscience*, 112.

170. August, 12, 1914, "Chicago Informant G," Charles E. Merriam Papers.

171. Ibid. For more on Alderman Abrahams, see *Chicago Daily Tribune*, "Manny Abrahams, Alderman, Dead," July 2, 1913, http://www. proquest.com (accessed January 23, 2012).

172. *Daily Jewish Forward*, March 23, 1924.

173. Ibid.

174. William G. Shepherd, "How to Make a Gangster," *Collier's Weekly*, September 2, 1933, 13. Historian Mark Haller also discusses the idea of hero worship in connection to crime, see Haller, "Ethnic Crime," 571–73.

175. Kraus, "Kosher Capones," 19.

176. *Chicago Daily Tribune*, "O'Banion Gang Like Pirates of Olden Days," November 11, 1924, http://www.proquest.com (accessed January 30, 2012).

177. *Chicago Daily Tribune*, "Marked Bills Trap Police in 'Dope' Plot," July 1, 1925, http://www.proquest.com (accessed January 30, 2012).

178. Landesco, *Organized Crime in Chicago*, 228.

179. Shepherd, "How to Make a Gangster," 12.

180. Ibid., 13.

181. Ibid.

CHAPTER 4

182. *Chicago Daily Tribune*, "Urges Jews to Combat Evil in Own Nationality," November 4, 1912, http://www.proquest.com (accessed February 1, 2012).

183. File #161: *People v. Phil Friedman*, Chicago Committee of Fifteen Records, Volume 25, Special Collections Research Center, University of Chicago Library. According to *Oxford English Dictionary* Online, "hustle" denotes engaging in prostitution.

184. Ibid.

185. Barnes, "Story of the Committee of Fifteen," 145. Barnes was an organizer and former president of the committee.

186. "Historical Note," Finding Aid for the Chicago Committee of Fifteen Records, Special Collections Research Center, University of Chicago Library.

187. *Social Evil in Chicago*, 25.

188. Ibid. See also "Historical Note." Mayor Harrison established the Morals Division after taking office in the fall of 1911.

189. This is similar to Brian Donovan's definition of white slavery, which he describes as "forced prostitution." See Donovan, *White Slave Crusades*, 1.

190. *Chicago Daily Tribune*, "Open War on Vice to Protect Girls," September 26, 1909, http://www.proquest.com (accessed February 1, 2012).

191. Asbury, *Gem of the Prairie*, 95–96.

192. Donovan, *White Slave Crusades*, 38.

193. Stead, *If Christ Came to Chicago*, 256.

194. Donovan, *White Slave Crusades*, 39.

195. Barnes, "Story of the Committee of Fifteen," 145.

196. Turner, "City of Chicago," 575.

197. Ibid., 581.

198. Ibid., 582.

199. Asbury, *Gem of the Prairie*, 266.

200. Turner, "City of Chicago," 582.

201. Barnes, "Story of the Committee of Fifteen," 146.

202. See *Daily Jewish Courier*, "The Fight Against 'White Slavery,'" November 5, 1907.

203. Ibid. Unfortunately, the CFLPS did not translate any more articles from Jewish periodicals in 1907 pertaining to white slavery, which is interesting in itself.

204. Ibid.

205. Cutler, *Jews of Chicago*, 164.

206. *Chicago Daily Tribune*, "Levee Seeks M'Cann's Scalp," April 18, 1908, http://www.proquest.com (accessed February 1, 2012).

207. *Chicago Daily Tribune*, "Appalling Discoveries by Government Agents," July 26, 1908, http://www.proquest.com (accessed February 1, 2012).

208. Ibid.

209. Donovan, *White Slave Crusades*, 31. *Chicago Daily Tribune* articles compared the problem of coerced prostitution to chattel slavery quite frequently.

210. Reckless, *Vice in Chicago*, 34.

211. Addams, *New Conscience*, 65–67.

212. Ibid., 154.

213. Abbott, *Sin in the Second City*, xxiv.

214. *Chicago Daily Tribune*, "Open War on Vice."

215. Blaustein and Blaustein, *Memoirs of David Blaustein*, 3.

216. Ibid., 181–87.

217. *Chicago Daily Tribune*, "Jews Preparing Roster of Vice," October 9, 1909, http://www.proquest.com (accessed February 1, 2012).

218. *Chicago Daily Tribune*, "Suit Over a Raid Amuses M'Cann," January 30, 1909, http://www.proquest.com (accessed February 1, 2012).

219. *Chicago Daily Tribune*, "Graft or a Plot? M'Cann Fight On," July 25, 1909, http://www.proquest.com (accessed February 2nd, 2012).

220. Ibid.

221. *Chicago Daily Tribune*, "Franks Confess in Detail," July 25, 1909, http://www.proquest.com (accessed February 2, 2012).

222. Ibid. For the artist's rendering of Louis Frank, see *Chicago Daily Tribune*, "Waiting to Be Called Before Grand Jury in Levee Inquiry," July 27, 1909, http://www.proquest.com (accessed April 2, 2012).

223. *Chicago Daily Tribune*, "Franks Confess in Detail."

224. *Chicago Daily Tribune*, "Repeat Blows at M'Cann," July 26, 1909, http://www.proquest.com (accessed February 2, 2012). For more on the Heitler connection, see Reckless, *Vice in Chicago*, 70, 83.

225. *Chicago Daily Tribune*, "Testimony Ends in M'Cann Trial," September 21, 1909, http://www.proquest.com (accessed February 2, 2012).

226. *Chicago Daily Tribune*, "Jail for M'Cann; Loses New Trial," October 29, 1910, http://www.proquest.com (accessed February 2, 2012).

227. *Chicago Daily Tribune*, "Churches Enter White Slave War," September 27, 1909, http://www.proquest.com (accessed February 2, 2012).

228. Cutler, *Jews of Chicago*, 33–34.

229. *Chicago Daily Tribune*, "Frank Brothers Spurned By Jews," September 25, 1909, http://www.proquest.com (accessed February 2, 2012).

230. Ibid.

231. *Chicago Daily Tribune*, "Open War on Vice."

232. Ibid.

233. *Social Evil in Chicago*, 288.

234. *Chicago Daily Tribune*, "Churches Enter White Slave War."

235. *Chicago Daily Tribune*, "Jews Smite Levee Traffic," October 4, 1909, http://www.proquest.com (accessed February 2, 2012).

236. The *Chicago Daily Tribune*'s October 17, 1909 article "Chicago's Civic Revolution" pictures David Blaustein, Adolf Kraus and Bernard Horwich (vice-president of the Hebrew Institute) alongside the likes of Jane Addams and Clifford Roe as the leaders of this movement.

237. *Jewish Advocate*, "War on the White Slave Traffic," October 15, 1909. http://www.proquest.com (accessed February 11, 2012).

238. *Chicago Daily Tribune*, "Jews Smite Levee Traffic."

239. *Chicago Daily Tribune*, "Jews Preparing Roster of Vice."

240. Donovan, *White Slave Crusades*, 1. See also Bell, *Fight the Traffic*, and Roe, *Panders and Their White Slaves*.

241. Ibid., 77.

242. Quoted in Knobel, *"America for the Americans,"* 224. See also the introduction in Gerber, *Anti-Semitism in American History*.

243. See the appendix for a selection of Jewish panderers.

244. Asbury, *Gem of the Prairie*, 285, 288.

245. *Social Evil in Chicago*, 227-8.

246. Reckless, *Vice in Chicago*, 5. See also Asbury, *Gem of the Prairie*, 287.

247. See *Social Evil in Chicago*, 57.

248. Reckless, *Vice in Chicago*, 3.

249. Ibid., 8.

250. *Daily Jewish Courier*, "Social Evil and the Jews," March 5, 1913.

251. Ibid.

252. *Daily Jewish Courier*, "Investigation Demanded for Ghetto District," July 20, 1913.

253. *Chicago Daily Tribune*, "Figures Reveal Big Increase in White Slavery," February 1, 1931, http://www.proquest.com (accessed March 25, 2012). This article specifically makes mention of Jewish gangster Harry Cusick (also spelled Guzik).

254. Asbury, *Gem of the Prairie*, 303.

255. On "historical amnesia," see Hayden, *Irish on the Inside*.

Chapter 5

256. *Daily Jewish Courier*, "There Is No Harm in Telling the Truth," July 17, 1914.

257. Several newspaper clippings verify that it was the same Frank brothers connected to the McCann trial. See *Chicago Daily Tribune*, "Clancy Cornered at M'Cann Trial," September 16, 1909, http://www.proquest.com (accessed February 22, 2012).

258. *Chicago Daily Tribune*, "Games Allowed to Run Openly," November 4, 1900, http://www.proquest.com (accessed February 7, 2012).

259. *Chicago Daily Tribune*, "Give Tiger Freer Rein," November 5, 1900, http://www.proquest.com (accessed February 22, 2012). In stud poker, according to *Oxford English Dictionary* Online, "the first card of a player's hand is dealt face down and the others face up, with betting after each round of the deal." Additionally, in draw poker, "each player is dealt five cards and, after the first round of betting, may discard some (usually up to three) of these cards and draw replacements from the dealer."

260. Ibid.

261. *Chicago Daily Tribune*, "Games Allowed to Run Openly."

262. Stead, *If Christ Came to Chicago*, 233–34.

263. *Chicago Daily Tribune*, "Games Allowed to Run Openly."

264. *Chicago Daily Tribune*, "From the Tribune's Columns," August 29, 1927, http://www.proquest.com (accessed February 22, 2012).

265. Landesco, *Organized Crime in Chicago*, 45.

266. *Illinois Gazette*, "Statutes Against Gaming," December 11, 1830, infotrac.galegroup.com (accessed February 24, 2012).

267. Asbury, *Gem of the Prairie*, 31–32.

268. Ibid., 33–36.

269. *Chicago Daily Tribune*, "Gambling," April 19, 1856, http://www.proquest.com (accessed February 22, 2012).

270. Thrasher, *The Gang*, 17.

271. Asbury, *Sucker's Progress*, 291.

272. Ibid., 300. See also Chafetz, *Play the Devil*, 270.

273. Asbury, *Sucker's Progress*, 299–300.

274. Ibid., 302. See also Stead, *If Christ Came to Chicago*, 234.

275. *Chicago Daily Tribune*, "The Civic Federation Gambling Report," September 22, 1894, http://www.proquest.com (accessed February 22, 2012). See also Lewis and Smith, *Chicago*, 236.

276. Ibid.

277. Asbury, *Sucker's Progress*, 305–06.

278. *Chicago Daily Tribune*, "Playing Policy All Over City," February 24, 1901, http://www.proquest.com (accessed February 22, 2012).

279. Ibid. See also Asbury, *Sucker's Progress*, 88–108.

280. *Chicago Daily Tribune*, "Playing Policy All Over City."

281. *Chicago Daily Tribune*, "Games Backed by Police," July 29, 1906, http://www.proquest.com (accessed February 22, 2012).

282. Jews founded the Chicago Hebrew Institute in 1903.

283. *Chicago Daily Tribune*, "'Wide Open' Spots in 'Closed Town,'" November 8, 1903, http://www.proquest.com (accessed February 22, 2012).

284. Ibid.

285. Landesco, *Organized Crime in Chicago*, 46.

286. Ibid., 46, 48.

287. *Chicago Daily Tribune*, "More Bombs for Gamblers," July 26, 1906, http://www.proquest.com (accessed February 22, 2012).

288. *Sentinel*, week of July 4, 1913.

289. *American Jewish Year Book*, September 9, 1907–September 25, 1908.

290. *Daily Jewish Courier*, "A Jew for Jews," April 1, 1910.

291. *Daily Jewish Courier*, "To the Jewish Voters of the 9th Ward," April 3, 1910.

292. *Chicago Daily Tribune*, "Games Backed by Police."

293. Landesco, *Organized Crime in Chicago*, 62. See also *Chicago Daily Tribune*, "New Slush Fund Stirs Police Body as Quiz Goes On," September 19, 1911, http://www.proquest.com (accessed February 22, 2012).

294. *Chicago Daily Tribune*, "Gambling Zones Ruled by Trio," September 15, 1911, http://www.proquest.com (accessed February 22, 2012).

295. *Chicago Daily Tribune*, "Gambling Inquiry May Hit 3 New District Rulers," September 16, 1911. http://www.proquest.com/ (accessed February 22, 2012). See also Landesco, *Organized Crime in Chicago*, 63.

296. *Chicago Daily Tribune*, "Charges Are Filed Against Revere, Baer and Hanley," November 23, 1911, http://www.proquest.com (accessed February 22, 2012).

297. Landesco, *Organized Crime in Chicago*, 62.

298. *Chicago Daily Tribune*, "Manny Abrahams, Alderman, Dead," July 2, 1913. See also Cutler, *Jews of Chicago*, 98.

299. *Chicago Daily Tribune*, "Thousands Attend Funeral of Ald. 'Manny' Abrahams," July 5, 1913, http://www.proquest.com (accessed February 22, 2012).

300. *Chicago Daily Tribune*, "Find Gambling; Man is Wounded," July 14, 1913, http://www.proquest.com (accessed February 22, 2012).

301. *Chicago Daily Tribune*, "Clamp Lid Tight on Gambling Dens," July 15, 1913, http://www.proquest.com (accessed February 22, 2012). This article includes an apparent transcript of the phone call.

302. Asbury, *Sucker's Progress*, 18. See also Merriam-Webster's dictionary entry for "stuss."

303. *Chicago Daily Tribune*, "Find Gambling; Man Is Wounded."

304. Courtesy of Google Maps.

305. See *Chicago Daily Tribune*, "Find Gambling; Man Is Wounded." The accompanying narrative, as well as all descriptions and language in quotations, are from this article's perspective.

306. See page 48.

307. Ibid. Bridewell was the city's penitentiary, located near Polk and Wells Streets. One of the gamblers, Ben Salin, lived with Belford at 1304 Newberry Avenue.

308. Ibid.

309. *Chicago Daily Tribune*, "Clamp Lid Tight on Gambling Dens."

310. *Chicago Daily Tribune*, "Revokes License of Gambling Den," July 16, 1913, http://www.proquest.com (accessed February 22, 2012).

311. *Chicago Daily Tribune*, "Clamp Lid Tight on Gambling Dens."

312. *Chicago Daily Tribune*, "Revokes License of Gambling Den."

313. Chicago Public Library Omnibus Project, *Bibliography of Foreign Language Newspapers*, 149.

314. Cutler, *Jews of Chicago*, 140–41.

315. *Daily Jewish Courier*, "Chief McWinney Declares That the Jewish Ghetto Is Free of Crime," July 23, 1913. The emphases are my own.

316. *Daily Jewish Courier*, "Investigation Demanded for Ghetto District," July 20, 1913.

317. *Daily Jewish Courier*, "There Is No Harm in Telling the Truth." Note that the CFLPS erroneously dates the editorial to 1914. Max Annenberg's trial concluded in October 1913. In this editorial, the author wrote, "The *Chicago Tribune*...in seeking to defend one of its employees who was accused of an 'attempt to kill' in the Saturday evening gun battle and held on $25,000 bond." Its language suggests an unresolved trial, so the date must be July 17, 1913.

318. Ibid. See also chapter one.

319. Ibid.

320. Ibid.

321. Ibid. It was perhaps no coincidence that the *Courier* specifically chose to mention Joseph Medill Elementary School, whose name honored the once co-owner of the *Chicago Daily Tribune*.

322. Ibid.

323. Known in Yiddish as *Tagliche Yiddische Presse*, the *Jewish Daily Press* was a conservative newspaper established in 1905. Its office was near Roosevelt Road and Throop Street. See Chicago Public Library Omnibus Project, *Bibliography of Foreign Language Newspapers*, 149.

324. *Jewish Daily Press*, "The Gamblers and Their Friends," July 17, 1913. Reprinted in *Chicago Daily Tribune*, July 20, 1913, http://www.proquest.com (accessed February 22, 2012).

325. *Daily Jewish Courier*, "There Is No Harm in Telling the Truth."

326. See *Chicago Daily Tribune*, "Tear Mask from Gambling," July 19, 1913, http://www.proquest.com (accessed February 22, 2012).

327. *Chicago Daily Tribune*, "Verdict Acquits Max Annenberg," October 8, 1913, http://www.proquest.com (accessed February 22, 2012).

328. August 5, 1914, "Case No. 2550: Chicago Informant B", Charles E. Merriam Papers.

329. December, 2, 1914, "Report of Number 100," Charles E. Merriam Papers.

CHAPTER 6

330. Dr. S.M. Melamed, "Good Morning," *Daily Jewish Courier*, April 10, 1923.

331. Landesco, *Organized Crime in Chicago*, 97–100.

332. Ibid., 237, 242. See also *Chicago Daily Tribune*, "Bootleg Feud Seen as Motive in New Murder," October 18, 1926, http://www.proquest.com (accessed February 26, 2012).

333. *Chicago Daily Tribune*, "Illinois Dry Chief Indicted in Wine Graft," July 24, 1925, http://www.proquest.com (accessed March 9, 2012).

334. *Chicago Daily Tribune*, "Chicago Seen as Mecca for Labor Grafters," November 27, 1927, http://www.proquest.com (accessed March 9, 2012).

335. Landesco, *Organized Crime in Chicago*, 146.

336. Cohen, *Racketeer's Progress*, 1.

337. Recall that the culture of Eastern European Jews centered on the home, synagogue and marketplace.

338. U.S. Constitution, amend. 16, sec. 1; Okrent, *Last Call*, 187; *Chicago Daily Tribune*, "Gibbons Take a Fall Out of 'Dry U.S.' Plan," January 21, 1919, http://www.proquest.com (accessed March 9, 2012).

339. Rabbi Leon Spitz, "Judaism and Prohibition," *Jewish Advocate*, May 16, 1930, http://www.proquest.com (accessed March 9, 2012).

340. Sprecher, "Let *Them* Drink," 135.

341. U.S. Constitution, amend. 16, sec. 6 quoted in Sprecher, "Let *Them* Drink," 135.

342. *Daily Jewish Courier*, "Government Concerns Itself with Kosher Wine," July 4, 1919.

343. *Sunday Jewish Courier*, "On the Community Stage," February 22, 1920.

344. *Chicago Daily Tribune*, "Orthodox Jews Get Ten Gallons of Wine Yearly," March 8, 1920, http://www.proquest.com (accessed March 9, 2012).

345. Asbury, *Great Illusion*, 239.

346. Sprecher, "Let *Them* Drink," 140.

347. Asbury, *Great Illusion, 239.*

348. *Chicago Defender*, "Ban on Sacrament Wine Lifted by Government," September 16, 1922. http://www.proquest.com (accessed March 9, 2012).

349. Among Chicago Jewry, the debate between sacramental wine and grape juice was already known.

350. Cutler, *Jews of Chicago*, 34.

351. *Chicago Daily Tribune*, "Rosenwald for Foregoing Wine at Sacrament," January 25, 1923, http://www.proquest.com (accessed March 9, 2012).

352. Julius Rosenwald, quoted in *Chicago Daily Tribune*, "Rosenwald for Foregoing Wine at Sacrament."

353. Ibid.

354. Julius Rosenwald, quoted in *Daily Jewish Courier*, "Rosenwald Fears Disgrace that May Be Caused by Sacramental Wine Business," January 25, 1923.

355. Julius Rosenwald, quoted in *New York Times*, "Ask Jews to Drop Yiddish and Wine," January 25, 1923, http://www.proquest.com (accessed March 9, 2012). The emphasis is my own.

356. Melamed, "Good Morning." See also Cutler, *Jews of Chicago*, 138–39.

357. Rabbi Margolis, quoted in *Jewish Advocate*, "Reform Rabbis Not Ones to Decide," February 1, 1923, http://www.proquest.com (accessed March 9, 2012).

358. *Daily Jewish Courier*, "How Much Is Two Times Two," September 8, 1921.

359. Baruch Sholom Levy, "About the Ivrith B-Ivrith and Ivrith Be-Yiddish Systems of Teaching," *Daily Jewish Courier*, February 5, 1922. See also Wirth, *Ghetto*, 248.

360. *Daily Jewish Courier*, "The Driving Force in Jewish Life," January 14, 1924. See also Okrent, *Last Call*, 187, and Joselit, *Our Gang*, 97.

361. *Chicago Daily Tribune*, "Grand Jury to Sift Graft in Wine Permits," September 26, 1924, http://www.proquest.com (accessed March 9, 2012).

362. U.S. Bureau of the Census, *Population 1920*, 48.

363. *Daily Jewish Forward*, "The New Scandal with the Sacramental Wine Business," February 23, 1926.

364. Edward Burns, "Wine Bootleggers," *Chicago Daily Tribune*, March 27, 1927, http://www.proquest.com (accessed March 9, 2012).

365. *Chicago Daily Tribune*, "Wine Graft 'King' Seized by U.S. Men," October 3, 1924, http://www.proquest.com (accessed March 9, 2012).

366. *Chicago Daily Tribune*, "New Wine List Brings Indicted Persons Up to 53," October 31, 1924, http://www.proquest.com (accessed March 9, 2012).

367. *Chicago Daily Tribune*, "Illinois Dry Chief Indicted in Wine Graft," July 24, 1925, http://www.proquest.com (accessed March 9, 2012).

368. *Daily Jewish Forward*, October 29, 1926. See also Burns, "Wine Bootleggers."

369. *Chicago Daily Tribune*, "Stone Testifies He Collected $34,000 Graft," October 27, 1927, http://www.proquest.com (accessed March 9, 2012).

370. *Daily Jewish Forward*, "The New Scandal with the Sacramental Wine Business."

371. Ibid.

372. Asbury, *Great Illusion*, 240.

373. *Chicago Daily Tribune*, "Move to Check Sacramental Wine Leakage," December, 2, 1925, http://www.proquest.com (accessed March 9, 2012).

374. Ibid.

375. *Chicago Daily Tribune*, "Cramton Bill Passes House," March 30, 1926, http://www.proquest.com (accessed March 9, 2012).

376. *Chicago Jewish Chronicle*, "The Need of a Kehillah in Chicago," week of December 30, 1927. For more on the history of the *kehillah*, see Elazar, *Kehillah*.

377. Cutler, *Jews of Chicago*, 285.

378. *Chicago Jewish Chronicle*, "The Need of a Kehillah in Chicago."

379. Cutler, *Jews of Chicago*, 285.

380. Fraser, *Labor Will Rule*, 5.

381. Cutler, *Jews of Chicago*, 184.

382. Fraser, *Labor Will Rule*, 36–39. See also Bisno, *Union Pioneer*.

383. *Daily Jewish Courier*, "Workers' Ghetto," September 15, 1914.

384. Cohen, *Racketeer's Progress*, 197.

385. *Daily Jewish Courier*, "In the Field of Labor," September 20, 1916.

386. Cutler, *Jews of Chicago*, 189.

387. Ibid.

388. Cohen, *Racketeer's Progress*, 198.

389. Ibid.

390. Ibid., 197.

391. Gorman and Miller were racketeers, respectively, in the laundry and cleaners and dryers industries. See *Chicago Daily Tribune*, "Hirschie Miller Quits Post with Laundry Ass'n," October 30, 1925, http://www.proquest.com (accessed March 15, 2012); *Chicago Daily Tribune*, "Capone's Cohorts Carry On," August 31, 1941; Landesco, *Organized Crime in Chicago*, 152–60.

392. Fraser, *Labor Will Rule*, 242.

393. Chicago Public Library Omnibus Project, *Bibliography of Foreign Language Newspapers*, 149. See Cohen, *Racketeer's Progress*, 201.

394. *World*, "Jewish Quarter Terrorized by Baker Bosses Association," October 19, 1917.

395. Ibid.

396. Ibid.

397. Ibid.

398. *World*, "Baker Trust Is Frightened," October 22, 1917.

399. *Chicago Daily Tribune*, "Price Cutting Baker Bombed," November 16, 1918, http://www.proquest.com (accessed March 12, 2012).

400. *Chicago Daily Tribune*, "'Plot' to Boost Bread Price in Wake of Strike," May 4, 1919, http://www.proquest.com (accessed March 9, 2012); *Chicago Daily Tribune*, "Women Riot as Bakers Increase Price of Bread," May 5, 1919.

401. *Chicago Daily Tribune*, "Police Shield Jewish Bakers from Crowds," June 15, 1927, http://www.proquest.com (accessed March 9, 2012).

402. *Chicago Daily Tribune*, "Bare High Fees Jewish Bakers Pay Organizers," November 17, 1927, http://www.proquest.com (accessed March 9, 2012).

According to James Barrett, the exacting of high fees was a common labor racketeering scheme.

403. *Chicago Daily Tribune*, "Chicago Seen as Mecca for Labor Grafters."

404. Ibid.; Landesco, *Organized Crime in Chicago*, 161–62; *Chicago Daily Tribune*, "Bomb Rocks Cooper-Carlton Hotel," December 13, 1927.

405. Masoudi, "Kosher Food Regulation," 668.

406. Ibid., 669.

407. Cohen, *Racketeer's Progress*, 198–99.

408. *Chicago Daily Tribune*, "50 True Bills Smash Bomb Terror Ring," December 5, 1925, http://www.proquest.com (accessed March 9, 2012).

409. Landesco, *Organized Crime in Chicago*, 160.

410. See ibid., 160–62.

411. *Chicago Daily Tribune*, "Threaten to Ban Jews' Meat in Row Over Eisen," October 10, 1931, http://www.proquest.com (accessed March 9, 2012).

412. *Chicago Daily Tribune*, "Stormy Session Over Eisen End with Phone Call," October 12, 1931, http://www.proquest.com (accessed March 9, 2012).

413. *Chicago Daily Tribune*, "Head of Kosher Butchers Held in 2 Bombings," September 4, 1932, http://www.proquest.com (accessed March 9, 2012).

414. *Chicago Daily Tribune*, "Chicken Killers Balk at Defense Fund for Etkin," June 22, 1929, http://www.proquest.com (accessed March 9, 2012).

415. Quoted in ibid.

416. *Chicago Daily Tribune*, "Rabbis Invoke Mosaic Law in War on Rackets," December 27, 1930, http://www.proquest.com (accessed March 9, 2012).

417. Ibid. The Talmud is the body of Jewish civil and ceremonial law.

418. Ibid.

419. *Chicago Daily Tribune*, "Orthodox Jews Press Fight on 'Racketeering' Shochtim," December 28, 1930, http://www.proquest.com (accessed March 9, 2012).

420. Ibid. Note Shochtim and *shochet* are, respectively, alternative spellings for *shochtem* and *schochet*.

421. Ibid. See also *Chicago Daily Tribune*, "Rabbis Invoke Mosaic Law in War on Rackets," December 27, 1930.

422. *Chicago Daily Tribune*, "Chicken Killers Strike in Reply to Ban of Rabbis," December 30, 1930, http://www.proquest.com (accessed March 9, 2012).

423. Ibid.

424. *Chicago Daily Tribune*, "Jews of Nation back Rabbis in War on Racket," December 31, 1930, http://www.proquest.com (accessed March 9, 2012). For more on Jewish racketeers in New York, see Joselit, *Our Gang*, 132–39.

425. *Chicago Daily Tribune*, "Rabbis Win War on Rackets," January 7, 1930, http://www.proquest.com (accessed March 9, 2012).

426. Ibid.

427. For the prevalence of bootlegging in sacramental wine among New York Jewry, see Sprecher, "Let *Them* Drink," 135–79; Joselit, *Our Gang*, 85–105. For their involvement in labor racketeering, see Joselit, *Our Gang*, 106–39.

CONCLUSION

428. Wirth, *Ghetto*, 263.

429. Cutler, *Jews of Chicago*, 101. Note that the near West Side, including the Maxwell Street ghetto, continued to be a classic area for immigrant settlement. Consequently, the decline of the ghetto refers specifically to the reduction of Jewish residents and institutions.

430. Wirth, *Ghetto*, 244. See also Cutler, *Jews of Chicago*, 99. Note that in both 1914 and 1920, the total enrollment was 1,200 pupils.

431. See map of synagogue distribution in Chicago below.

432. Cutler, *Jews of Chicago*, 88.

433. Federal Works Agency, *Bibliography of Foreign Language Newspapers*, 149.

434. Cutler, *Jews of Chicago*, 141.

435. Wirth, *Ghetto*, 250.

436. Cutler, *Jews of Chicago*, 141.

437. Wirth, *Ghetto*, 62.

438. George Bliss, "Guzik Death May Not Halt His Law Suits," *Chicago Daily Tribune*, February 23, 1956, http://www.proquest.com (accessed March 27, 2012).

439. *Chicago Daily Tribune*, "Gang Chief Guzik Dies," February 22, 1956, http://www.proquest.com (accessed March 27, 2012).

440. Ibid.

441. "Notice of Levy," June 7, 1939, Arthur W. Mitchell Papers, 1898–1968.

442. Ibid. See also Kraus, "Kosher Capones," 338–43.

443. *Chicago Daily Tribune*, "Jack Guzik Now Is No. 1 Man of Gang Overlords," October 25, 1941, http://www.proquest.com (accessed March 27, 2012).

444. *Chicago Daily Tribune*, "Guzik Threatens Law Suit If Arlington Park Bars Him," July 24, 1954, http://www.proquest.com (accessed March 27, 2012).

445. Ibid.

446. *Chicago Daily Tribune*, "400 Mourners Pass Gangster Guzik's Body," February 24, 1956, http://www.proquest.com (accessed March 27, 2012).

BIBLIOGRAPHY

PRIMARY SOURCES

Newspapers

American Jewish Yearbook, 1907–8. Translated and edited by the Chicago Public Library Omnibus Project. Chicago Foreign Language Press Survey. http://www.archive.org/search.php?query=title%3A%22Chicago%20 Foreign%20Language%20Press%22 [Unless otherwise noted, this is the URL to the subsequent newspapers.]

Chicago Daily Tribune, 1856–1956. http://www.proquest.com.

Chicago Hebrew Institute Observer, 1918–19. Translated and edited by the Chicago Public Library Omnibus Project. Chicago Foreign Language Press Survey.

Chicago Jewish Chronicle, 1924–27. Translated and edited by the Chicago Public Library Omnibus Project. Chicago Foreign Language Press Survey.

Daily Jewish Courier, 1907–24. Translated and edited by the Chicago Public Library Omnibus Project. Chicago Foreign Language Press Survey.

Daily Jewish Forward, 1924–26. Translated and edited by the Chicago Public Library Omnibus Project. Chicago Foreign Language Press Survey.

Illinois Gazette, 1830. Infotrac.galegroup.com.

Illinois Staats-Leitung, 1901. Translated and edited by the Chicago Public Library Omnibus Project. Chicago Foreign Language Press Survey.

Jewish Advocate, 1909–30. http://www.proquest.com.

Sentinel, 1913. Translated and edited by the Chicago Public Library Omnibus Project. Chicago Foreign Language Press Survey.

Sunday Jewish Courier, 1920–24. Translated and edited by the Chicago Public Library Omnibus Project. Chicago Foreign Language Press Survey.

World, 1917. Translated and edited by the Chicago Public Library Omnibus Project. Chicago Foreign Language Press Survey.

Other Primary Sources

Bell, Ernest A. *Fight the Traffic in Young Girls*. N.p.: G.S. Ball, 1910.

Bennett, James O'Donnell. *Chicago Gangland*. Chicago: Tribune Co., 1929.

"'Chicago. 2000':1." 1910. C.S. Hammond & Company Atlas. United States Digital Map Library. http://usgwarchives.net/maps/usa/hammonds1910/index.html/ (accessed November 13, 2011).

Chicago Committee of Fifteen Records. Vol. 25. Special Collections Research Center, University of Chicago Library.

Flynt, Josiah. "In the World of Graft: 'Chi,' an Honest City." *McClure's* 16 (November 1900–April 1901).

Gerage, Nick. *A Map of Chicago's Gangland, from Authentic Sources*. 48 x 62 cm. Chicago: Nick Gerage, 1900–93.

Papers, 1893–1957. Charles Edward Merriam. University of Chicago Library, Chicago.

Papers, 1898–1968. Arthur W. Mitchell. Box 48, Folder 10. Chicago History Museum, Chicago.

Roe, Clifford G. *Panders and Their White Slaves*. New York: F.H. Revell, 1910.

Shepherd, William G. "How to Make a Gangster." *Collier's Weekly*, September 2, 1933.

The Social Evil in Chicago: A Study of Existing Conditions with Recommendations by the Vice Commission of Chicago. Chicago: Gunthorp-Warren Printing Company, 1911.

Stead, William T. *If Christ Came to Chicago: A Plea for the Union of All Who Love in the Service of All Who Suffer*. Chicago: Laird and Lee, 1894.

Thrasher, Frederic. *The Gang: A Study of 1,313 Gangs in Chicago*. 1927. Reprint, Chicago: University of Chicago Press, 1936.

Turner, George Kibbe. "The City of Chicago: A Study of the Great Immoralities." *McClure's* (April 1907).

U.S. Bureau of the Census. *Population 1920: General Report and Analytical Tables, prepared under the supervision of William C. Hunt, chief statistician for population*. Washington, D.C.: Government Printing Office, 1922.

Secondary Sources

Abbott, Edith. *The Tenements of Chicago, 1908–1935*. 1936. Reprint, New York: Arno Press, Inc., 1970.

Abbott, Karen. *Sin in the Second City: Madams, Ministers, Playboys, and the Battle For America's Soul*. New York: Random House, 2007.

Addams, Jane. *A New Conscience and an Ancient Evil*. 1912. Reprint, New York: Arno Press, 1972.

Asbury, Herbert. *Gem of the Prairie: An Informal History of the Chicago Underworld*. New York: Alfred A. Knopf, Inc., 1940.

————. *The Great Illusion: An Informal History of Prohibition*. Garden City, NY: Doubleday & Company, Inc., 1950.

————. *Sucker's Progress: An Informal History of Gambling in America from the Colonies to Canfield*. Montclair, NJ: Patterson Smith, 1969.

Barnes, Clifford W. "The Story of the Committee of Fifteen of Chicago." *Journal of Social Hygiene* 4 (April 1918): 145–56.

Benton, Colbee C. *Prairie State: Impressions of Illinois, 1673–1967, Travelers and Other Observers*. Edited by Paul M. Angle. Chicago: University of Chicago Press, 1968.

Bisno, Abraham. *Union Pioneer*. Madison: University of Wisconsin Press, 1967.

Blaustein, Miriam Umstadter, and David Blaustein. *Memoirs of David Blaustein, Educator and Communal Worker*. New York: McBride, Nast and Co., 1913.

Bregstone, Philip P. *Chicago and Its Jews*. Chicago: privately published, 1933.

Butler, Charles. *As Others See Chicago: Impressions of Visitors, 1673–1933*. Edited by Bessie Louise Pierce. Chicago: University of Chicago Press, 2004.

Chafetz, Henry. *Play the Devil: A History of Gambling in the United States from 1492 to 1955*. New York: Clarkson N. Potter, Inc., 1960.

Chicago Public Library Omnibus Project. Bibliography of Foreign Language Newspapers and Periodicals Published in Chicago. Chicago, 1942.

Cohen, Andrew Wender. *The Racketeer's Progress: Chicago and the Struggle for the Modern American Economy, 1900–1940*. Cambridge, UK: Cambridge University Press, 2004.

Cohen, Rich. *Tough Jews: Fathers, Sons and Gangster Dreams*. New York: Simon & Schuster, 1998.

Cutler, Irving. *The Jews of Chicago: From Shtetl to Suburb.* Rev. ed. Urbana: University of Illinois Press, 2009.

Diamond, Andrew J. *Mean Streets: Chicago Youths and the Everyday Struggle for Empowerment in the Multiracial City, 1908–1969.* Berkeley: University of California Press, 2009.

Donovan, Brian. *White Slave Crusades: Race Gender and Anti-Vice Activism, 1887–1997.* Urbana: University of Illinois Press, 2006.

Elazar, Daniel Judah. *The Kehillah.* Ramat-Gan: Bar-Ilan University, 1977.

Fraser, Steven. *Labor Will Rule: Sidney Hillman and the Rise of American Labor.* New York: Free Press, 1991.

Gerber, David A. *Anti-Semitism in American History.* Urbana: University of Illinois Press, 1987.

Goren, Arthur A. *New York Jews and the Quest for Community: The Kehillah Experiment, 1908–1922.* New York: Columbia University Press, 1970.

Haller, Mark H. "Ethnic Crime: The Organized Underworld of Early 20th Century Chicago." In *Ethnic Chicago: A Multicultural Portrait*, edited by Melvin G. Holli and Peter d'A. Jones, 557–73. Grand Rapids, MI: Wm. B. Eerdmans Publishing Co., 1995.

———. "Organized Crime in Urban Society: Chicago in the Twentieth Century." *Journal of Social History* 5, no. 2 (Winter 1971–72): 210–34.

Hansen, Marcus Lee. "The Problem of the Third Generation Immigrant." In *American Immigrants and Their Generations: Studies and Commentaries on the Hansen Thesis After Fifty Years*, edited by Peter Kivisto and Dag Blanck, 191–203. Urbana: University of Illinois Press, 1990.

Hayden, Tom. *Irish on the Inside: In Search of the Soul of Irish America.* New York: Verso, 2001.

Henry Justin Smith, and Lloyd Lewis. *Chicago: The History of Its Reputation.* New York: Harcourt, Brace and Company, 1929.

Holland, Robert. *Chicago in Maps*. New York: Rizzoli, 2005.

Joselit, Jenna Weissman. *Our Gang: Jewish Crime and the New York Jewish Community, 1900–1940*. Bloomington: Indiana University Press, 1983.

Knobel, Dale T. *"America for the Americans": The Nativist Movement in the United States*. New York: Twayne Publishers, 1996.

Korey, Harold. "The History of Jewish Education in Chicago." PhD diss., University of Chicago, Department of Education, 1942.

Kraus, Joe. "The Jewish Gangster: A Conversation Across Generations." *American Scholar* 84 (Winter 1995): 53–65.

———. "The Kosher Capones: Recovering the History of Chicago's Jewish Gangsters." Ms., University of Scranton, 2007.

Lait, Jack, and Lee Mortimer. *Chicago: Confidential!* New York: Crown Publishers, 1950.

Landesco, John. "Crime and the Failure of Institutions in Chicago's Immigrant Areas." *Journal of Criminal Law and Criminology* 23, no. 2 (July–August 1932): 238–48.

———. *Organized Crime in Chicago: Part III of the Illinois Crime Survey, 1929*. 1929. Reprint, Chicago: University of Chicago Press, 1968.

Levine, Bruce. *The Spirit of 1848: German Immigrants, Labor Conflict and the Coming of the Civil War*. Urbana: University of Illinois Press, 1992.

Masoudi, Gerald F. "Kosher Food Regulation and the Religion Clauses of the First Amendment." *University of Chicago Law Review* 60, no. 2 (Spring, 1993): 667–96.

Mazur, Edward Herbert. "Minyans for a Prairie City: The Politics of Chicago Jewry 1850–1940." PhD diss., University of Chicago, 1974.

Meites, Hyman Louis. *History of the Jews of Chicago*. Chicago: Jewish Historical Society of Illinois, 1924.

Murray, George. *The Madhouse on Madison Street*. Chicago: Follett Publishing Company, 1965.

O'Kane, James M. *The Crooked Ladder: Gangsters, Ethnicity, and the American Dream*. New Brunswick, NJ: Transaction Publishers, 1992.

Okrent, Daniel. *Last Call: The Rise and Fall of Prohibition*. New York: Scribner, 2010.

Polacheck, Hilda Satt. *I Came a Stranger: The Story of a Hull-House Girl*. Urbana: University of Illinois Press, 1991.

Reckless, Walter C. *Vice in Chicago*. Chicago: University of Chicago Press, 1933.

Reitman, Ben L. *The Second Oldest Profession: A Study of the Prostitute's "Business Manager."* New York: Vanguard Press, 1931.

Ruth, David E. *Inventing the Public Enemy: The Gangster in American Culture, 1918–1934*. Chicago: University of Chicago Press, 1996.

Sentinel. *History of Chicago Jewry, 1911–1961*. Chicago: Sentinel Publishing Co., 1961.

Spinney, Robert G. *City of Big Shoulders: A History of Chicago*. DeKalb: Northern Illinois University Press, 2000.

Sprecher, Hannah. "Let *Them* Drink and Forget Our Poverty: Orthodox Rabbis React to Prohibition." *American Jewish Archives* 2 (Fall/Winter 1991): 135–79.

Tebbel, John. *The American Magazine: A Compact History*. New York: Hawthorn Books, Inc., 1969.

Wendt, Lloyd, and Herman Kogan. *Lords of the Levee: The Story of Bathhouse John and Hinky Dink*. Cornwall, UK: Cornwall Press, 1943.

Wirth, Louis. *The Ghetto*. 1928. Reprint, Chicago: University of Chicago Press, 1956.

INDEX

Index

ABOUT THE AUTHOR

Alex Garel-Frantzen is a student at the University of Illinois College of Law, where he is a juris doctor candidate set to graduate in 2015. He is a three-time winner of the CALI Award for earning the highest score in law school courses relating to legal research and writing and is a member of the *University of Illinois Law Review*.

Alex earned a BA in history with a minor in Spanish in May 2012 from the University of Illinois at Champaign-Urbana, where he completed his degree in three years and graduated magna cum laude with highest distinction. He was awarded the Department of History Scholarship for Outstanding Senior Honors Thesis and the Martha Belle Barrett Scholarship for Undergraduate Academic Excellence and superior commitment to the study of history. Alex is also a member of Phi Beta Kappa, the nation's oldest academic honor society.

In his spare time, Alex enjoys spending time with family (including the doggies) and friends, exercising, playing guitar and volunteering.

He is a resident of Buffalo Grove, a northwest suburb of Chicago.